The Secrets of Immortality

Endorsements for
The Secrets of Immortality

I absolutely loved Dr. Schwarz's point of view about the science and religion world working together. Truthfully and honestly exploring the unexplainable energetic phenomenons that occur regularly in life, including the ones witnessed in the scientific medical field. We all have experienced mysterious energies. The exploration of immortality from a bio scientific and spiritual-theological view is an extraordinary approach. I hope *The Secrets of Immortality* opens up an honest dialogue in the future.

—**Kelly L. Carlson,**
Actress, Los Angeles, USA

The Secrets of Immortality is an amazing book with unique perspectives for the eternal human quest of immortality.

—**Parag Bharadwaj, MD,**
Palliative Care Director, Irvine, USA

If we consider that survival is the common denominator in all religions, and science, I find Dr. Ernst von Schwarz's scientific approach for optimal expansion of life and the theological aspect of immortality are informative and very fascinating to say the least.

—**Sofia Milos,**
Actress, Los Angeles, USA & Rome, Italy

This book is a valuable resource for medical professionals, clergy, and philosophers seeking expert advice and reflections on how to deal with people's hopes and fears regarding immortality and eternal life.

—**Laurent Cleenewerk, PhD,**
Professor of Theology, Euclid University, Washington D.C., USA

Dr. Ernst von Schwarz has tackled the subject of immortality based on two often conflicting perspectives, science/medicine, and religion. As a practicing physician, innovative scientist, as well as an academic theologian and Roman Catholic, Dr. Schwarz provides a very unique but methodological perspective on the prolongation of life, the meaning of death, and our search for immortality. As a scientist and Catholic myself, I find *The Secrets of Immortality* a thought provoking book.

—Nathan S. Bryan, PhD,
Professor of Molecular Medicine, University of Texas, Houston, USA

The Secrets of Immortality is an interesting book on thoughts and scientific approaches to eternal life. The philosophical and theological aspects of immortality are explained by a medical scientist who is involved in research, and who is also an academic Roman Catholic theologian.

—Frank G. Mancuso,
Studio Executive, Los Angeles, USA

The Secrets of Immortality offers a fascinating exploration of existential puzzlements about the goals of medicine, the possibilities and limits of technological power, and the finitude of the human condition. A well-argued and highly recommended book, which crosses disciplinary boundaries between science and the humanities, too often kept separate. A display of speculative daring, informed by intellectual courage.

—Roberto Dell'Oro, PhD,
Professor and O'Malley Chair in Bioethics,
Loyola Marymount University, Los Angeles, USA

THE SECRETS OF Immortality

A SCIENTIFIC AND THEOLOGICAL APPROACH TO EVERLASTING LIFE

PROF. DR. ERNST VON SCHWARZ

NEW YORK

LONDON • NASHVILLE • MELBOURNE • VANCOUVER

The Secrets of Immortality

A Scientific and Theological Approach to Everlasting Life

Published in New York, New York, by Morgan James Publishing. Morgan James is a trademark of Morgan James, LLC. www.MorganJamesPublishing.com

Proudly distributed by Publisher's Group West.

Dr. Ernst von Schwarz, MD, PhD, is a practicing heart transplant and interventional cardiologist, scientist, and Professor of Medicine in Los Angeles, California. Dr. Schwarz is a world-renowned pioneer in stem cell research and has published more than 150 scientific articles and several book chapters and books in Cardiovascular Medicine, lastly *The Secret World of Stem Cell Therapy – What YOU need to know about the Health, Beauty, and Anti-Aging Breakthrough*, Morgan James Publishing, New York, 2022. He also studied Roman Catholic Theology and earned his doctorate in Roman Catholic Theology in 2022, and is also a Professor of Bioethics at Euclid University, an Intergovernmental Institution under United Nations Treaty 49006/49007.

Medicine, medical sciences and advances in biotechnology as well theological interpretations are in constant flux. The statements made in this book represent the personal opinion of the author Dr. Ernst von Schwarz but do not replace any recommendations or prescriptions from any healthcare professional to any patient. In addition, the statements do not represent a complete review of the current scientific data on medicine or theology on the topics discussed, but a personal view on scientific facts and writings to the best of the Dr. Ernst von Schwarz's knowledge at the time of writing. Moreover, statements on faith and theology do not represent the view of the Catholic Church or any other church but solely the author's personal views.

Morgan James BOGO™

A **FREE** ebook edition is available for you or a friend with the purchase of this print book.

CLEARLY SIGN YOUR NAME ABOVE

Instructions to claim your free ebook edition:
1. Visit MorganJamesBOGO.com
2. Sign your name CLEARLY in the space above
3. Complete the form and submit a photo of this entire page
4. You or your friend can download the ebook to your preferred device

ISBN 9781636980805 paperback
ISBN 9781636980812 ebook
Library of Congress Control Number: 2022948092

Cover & Interior Design by:
Christopher Kirk
www.GFSstudio.com

with...

Morgan James is a proud partner of Habitat for Humanity Peninsula and Greater Williamsburg. Partners in building since 2006.

Get involved today! Visit: www.morgan-james-publishing.com/giving-back

Dedicated to
My beloved wife Angela Oakenfold von Schwarz

Table Of Contents

Foreword

In *The Secrets of Immortality*, Dr Ernst von Schwarz does not aim to present a secret medical treatment to achieve personal immortality or super-longevity. Rather, his goal is much more informative and ultimately valuable, especially for those of us who often reflect on the mystery of death (physicians and clergy) but also the human quest to deal with mortality and never-dying hope for some kind of immortality.

This being said, Dr Schwarz is able to share his knowledge both as a practicing cardiologist and theologian including on cutting edge topics such as gene reprogramming and regenerative medicine.

This remarkable book is also very personal and therefore multifaceted; many readers will connect with the author's reflections and quest for rational and scientific answers. It is a rare invitation to explore the secrets thoughts of immortality that whisper with us and have done so throughout human history. It is also an opportunity for all readers, especially faith-seeking readers, to reflect on the state of conflict or harmony between science (including medicine) and faith (notably historic Christianity).

Last but not least, this book is a valuable resource for medical professions, clergy and bioethicists seeking expert advice and reflections on to deal with people's hopes and fears related to mortality and 'eternal life.'

Dr Ernst von Schwarz contribution here is a tour de force of interdisciplinary research, which is both accessible and rigorous, academic yet solidly grounded in a doctor's lifelong experience dealing with life and death.

Pr Laurent Cleenewerck de Kiev, California

Preface

As a physician, Doctor of Medicine, clinical researcher and scientist I have been involved in groundbreaking research in innovative and regenerative medicine (in contrast to the traditional reactive medicine) including stem cell research over the last 20 years. With the option to regenerate damaged or aging organs and tissue, the quest for longer-lasting life, health care rather than sick care, longevity, and even immortality is more apparent now than ever. There are several reasons since medicine and science both give humankind the hope of longevity based on advances in technology and therapy. This is true in particular for cardiovascular diseases, which represent the number one causes of mortality everywhere in the world.

At the edge of scientific advances there always appears the philosophical question whether we as human beings really should want to gain ever-lasting life or whether our personal goals should be more in terms of longing for a longer but healthier existence, instead. Over the last century, biological sciences and especially medical sciences have taken over the leading role of thought and studies over the former supremacy of theology and philosophy in academic intellectualism. However, as a physician and scientist, I naturally had to come to the conclusion that the incomprehensible phenomenon of the existence of God as the creator and mover of our earthly life and beyond is at least as important (if not more) in the quest for immortality as hoping for and trusting advances in biotechnological research.

There are several questions with regard to men's continuous quest for immortality which appears to be as old as human thinking and seems to be integral to human nature. The first question remains: is immortality feasible? If so, will humankind then ever be able to find a path to biologic immortality? And if this would be possible, then the next question is whether we really want to be immortal, from personal, ethical, theological, sociological, anthropological, economical, and even political points of view.

The more modern biotechnological science is able to teach us and the more we learn about intracellular pathways and biochemical reactions that lead to processes of senescence (cell aging), the more efficiently we are able to develop adequate interventions either to pause these processes or to even to prevent them in its entirety. Looking into nature and observing reptiles replacing entire limbs after traumatic amputation or visualizing jelly fishes appearing indestructible by age or disease, we wonder why the most specialized species on earth, namely us humans, did lose so many of our basic biologic survival mechanisms throughout evolution. If a jelly fish can reproduce itself forever, why should we as human beings and the highest developed species on earth at the current time not be able to replicate these simple mechanisms leading to reversing of aging and becoming immortal? Jelly fishes are very complex rather than simple organisms, but in the history of life, they are definitely not as complex as the human species. We humbly do not have the correct answers, yet.

Looking at our own bodies as a doctor of medicine, I have learned that there are some organs that have the capability to regenerate portions of their material and functional structure after those have been damaged and lost, usually as a result of external trauma or disease. The reason for this regenerative ability is the existence of dormant organ-based stem cells, and some of our organs and tissues do have a large number of these repair units in storage. This stem cell reservoir has the potency to reproduce tissues and cells that have been injured or killed. In particular our liver and our skin have these regenerative powers. If we cut off portions of our liver, the remaining organ is able to rebuild whatever it takes to fulfill all of its metabolic and cleansing tasks for our body. In addition, our skin is able to rebuild damaged skin, at least in part (we might develop a scar composed of stiff connective tissue, but the skin heals itself relatively well). Unfortunately, this amazing ability to regenerate is not available in many other organs such as the most important ones for survival, namely the heart or the brain. This is a problem since life is absolutely dependent on the vital functions of the heart, i.e., the pumping of blood in order to ensure the perfusion of the complete body with oxygen and metabolites and its metabolic waste removal. If the heart stops its pumping function, then there is no circulation in our body within a few seconds, and we die instantaneously, usually within minutes. If our brains do not work, then we might be in a vegetative state without the capabilities to effectively interact with our environments. Furthermore, once brain death occurs, even if our heart still pumps or our lungs are still artificially ventilated, we also die.

Modern medicine has more evolved over the last 100 years than ever before, and modern biotechnology has become the target of hope and dreams among the public based on publicized study results of anti-aging mechanisms and genetic manipulation, even if these were just obtained from in vitro cell cultures studies or in vivo rodent experiments (rather than from human clinical trials). Various industries now have initiated major funding using hundreds of millions of dollars to search for the fountain of youth and for everlasting life. Futurists calculate the speed of further discovery until humankind becomes immortal and even a new species, a combination between man and machine, human and computer will develop, as the trans-humanist movement believes in.

There is a huge number of recent publications - especially books - on immortality and on not-dying, including several declared attempts to defy death by means of modern technology. Of interest, most of these publications are not authored by scientists or basic researchers, and especially not be clinical physicians, but rather by lay people interested in the topic. This is not surprising, since basic researchers usually spend their time in the experimental laboratories conducting their research and trying to publish it accordingly in peer-reviewed scientific journals that usually are only read by their peer scientists working on similar topics in the same fields.

Clinical doctors are ordinarily pre-occupied with their daily routine, dealing with sick patients requiring their utmost attention, and are consequently subjugated with whatever medicine can offer today to treat these diseases. Practical clinical medicine, unfortunately for many, is oftentimes somewhat distinctly distant from those promising advances coming freshly out of the experimental research laboratories. Universally, there is a huge discrepancy between basic research accomplishments and practiced clinical healthcare in medicine, which scholars tried to overcome by introducing the term *translational medicine*, which is supposed to enable a flawless transition between basic research findings and clinical medicine. This, however, is almost never feasible in today's world. Even if there might be new drugs and technologies that have shown promising results in experimental animals, there is still a long way from the animal lab to clinical use in human patients. Even if it would be feasible to use a new drug in a patient in whom all standard treatments fail, then no insurance company would pay for an experimental approach, and patient would have to pay out of pocket for un-approved therapies, which in itself bares serval medical legal issues. On the other hand, several therapies that work might take a long time to be officially approved, in the US meaning *FDA-approved*. The use of stents for blockages of arteries in the heart that we are deploying every single day since approximately 35 years, were not approved by the FDA for many years after they were introduced (and used by cardiologists all over), as an example. Even if there is an innovative approach seen in the experimental setting, it might take decades before such inventions can be available for a large group of patients for medical use.

The only example to the contrary of the usual delays from bench to bedside was the enormous fast discovery, development and production of mRNA-based vaccines for COVID-19 in 2020 by certain pharma concerns such as Pfizer and Moderna, that - for the sake of saving millions of lives form a deadly virus – in fact did receive an unprecedented fast emergent use FDA-approval.

Besides appropriate medical care, religious beliefs, on the other hand, have an enormous impact on the physical and psychological well-being of most individuals, often dependent on their cultural backgrounds or upbringing. Even without any formal religious community belonging or teachings, many have some kind of personal (or anonymous) spiritual sense and beliefs that clearly do affect their psychological, social, and physical subsistence. The enigmatic human mind has an enormous effect on how a person experiences changes in life, diseases, sufferings, healing or even the acceptance of incurable conditions, until death. As physicians, we oftentimes do not pay enough attention to the power of the mind and spirit as part of a holistic management of any particular individual, but we are surprised how different outcomes might be whether or not someone believes in God or in any higher power. The physician's role is of essential significance for the care of any patient, and we all are patients, sooner or later. Whether or not the patients believe in a higher power, in any case the physician–patient relationship is of enormous importance to create a trusting interaction between the sick and the healer, whereas the healer many times might not be able to cure but is rather a supportive agent to manage the diseased.

Besides the individual fate and beliefs and questions and hopes for anyone's individual life and health and fate, there is a public world that does not accept religion in view of modern science. It appears to be opinion for many that people of faith seem to be like in one of the best movies of all times, the turk Sollozzo talked to Michael Corleone about his father Don Vito: "...ma tu patri pensa all'antica" (The Godfather, by Francis Ford Coppola, 1972), and as a result, people of religious faith feel a bit lost in the context of scientific discussions, and modern scientists are mainly atheists in nature. Religious beliefs appear outdated, antique, old-fashioned, even ridiculous, and in complete contrast to the advances in modern science, according to many. Science is explaining the world as it is, by use of analytical technology and reproducible experiments, in which faith has no place to exist. On the other hand, some believe that faith and science are enemies by nature, and science makes faith obsolete, while religion in general is against evolution and adheres to whatever is written in the old bible as the only truth.

Nothing could be more far from the truth. Despite its controverse history, I strongly believe that faith and science can be complementary. I will try to show the reader how science and faith can interact in a mutual beneficial way rather than opposing each other. The reason to do so, for me personally, is the fact the medicine did lead me to my faith.

By the way, Sollozzo wanted to be modern and progressive and tried to convince the old-fashioned Don Corleone to help him to establish a business of narcotics dealing with the Tattaglia family which the Godfather refused, but then Sollozzo was killed by Vito's son Michael, in the movie.

I do not have all the answers (and I guess, nobody does), but at one day, I hope to be able to say "I do not seek, I find" (*Pablo Picasso, 1936*).

Professor Dr. Ernst von Schwarz, Los Angeles

Introduction

I n present days, health care providers thrive on the dilemma of maximum care based available technologies and advances in modern medicine versus the ethical dilemma of accepting an impending end of life and possibly withdrawing care in cases of medical futility, where all medical means are not anymore able to help or prevent decline of health and death. Due to populistic ideas of biologic immortality, believe in a futuristic immortal existence due to modern computing and biotechnology oftentimes replaces religious faith in an everlasting life after death, which might lead to unrealistic patient expectations, oftentimes beyond medical possibilities.

Regardless of the cultural background and difference, people across the globe aspire for an illness-free life, better yet, living life with utmost care-free quality. Immortality can be an answer when defined either by living forever young or by living a life with supreme standards, especially regarding one's health. The purpose of this work is to impart knowledge on the religious beliefs of immortality and its alignments with today's medical advancements that are in purge to ailment-free longevity existence. In due for this study literature searches were done on various databases including, JSTOR, PubMed, and numerous sacred religions scriptures. After extensive research on immortality in religious as well as medical perspectives it appears that most religions believe in some sort of immortality, afterlife or reincarnation, and the soul is ultimately considered as immortal. Despite a growing rate and propagation of atheism among scientists, advances in modern medicine achieving prolongation of life and improved survival rates for many diseases do not need to contradict the Christian faith in immortality of the soul and the resurrection after death. Science explores how things are happening by use of reproducible experimental settings, but it cannot understand why the mystery of life on earth, our existence and our consciousness occur. Religion on the other hand, provides the basis for the faith of why things are happening and why we are alive and conscious. The focus for Christianity is the acceptance of God as the creator of all things and Jesus of Nazareth as the Christ, the Anointed one of God. Christianity represents a living tradition of faith, a culture and a way of life based on sacred scripture and sacred tradition. Philosophical, religious, scientific and populistic writings are critically evaluated to demonstrate that religion does accept science and science does not contradict Christian doctrines. As such, health care providers do not need to compromise their own religious faith or the faith of their patients by using biotechnologic advances by treating life threatening illnesses. While modern medicine and biotechnology does provide advances to prolong life, the medicine for true immortality to achieve resurrection after death represents the basic for Christian faith with the belief in the Eucharist. As such, a theologic approach to medicine might be beneficial for holistic patient care management.

The quest for immortality exists since mankind exists, at least so we do believe. The facts are, however, that despite all attempts, not one single person on earth has ever become immortal, and except the 7.9 billion human beings who are alive in our known world at the current time, everyone else has died, so far, including the scientists who worked on anti-aging or immortality, including kings and queens and priests and all the former Popes, and even Jesus Christ died on the cross.

The question remains, however, whether our biologic clock and our nature could ever be reprogrammed to achieve immortality. At the least, we are trying to prolong life by defying diseases. We will discuss the aspects of immortality from a medical/biologic point of view as well as from a philosophical/theological aspect and we might understand, that some form of immortality will be possible.

Chapter One

The Dilemma

A s a Christian and a physician, I myself as well as many if not most of my colleagues are faced on a daily base with the reality of mortality on one side and the aspiration of immortality on the other side. We as physicians and even more in our position as researchers share the enlightening experiences and flashbacks after coming back from scientific conferences where we hear about innovative technologic advances in modern medicine to ensure higher quality imaging, to better and earlier detect micro-damage of heart muscle cells, or to use high tech electrical microtransducers to stimulate certain organ structures – just to give a few examples.

Sitting at the bedside of a patient with end-stage heart disease or cancer during his last days of life a few days after such as conference, however, does represent a completely different scenario in which we as doctors practicing medicine know very well that none of the new developments we just have encountered at that interesting last conference will change a thing in the course of the disease and the natural course of life for this particular individual, who likely is going to die within the next days. The physician knows it, but the family and the patient might be on denial. There is no miracle drug we can offer, there is no surgical procedure at this stage that would change things around, it is at a certain point, too late in the game to unwind the biological clock, at least for most cases.

I have experienced many situations where relatives came to me and asking about something they read on the internet which can "reverse the blocked arteries" or "a new chemotherapeutic agent that will kill all cancer cells with no side effects". We have to remind ourselves in those situations that - first of all - Dr. Google is neither a physician, nor anyone who ever treated a patient, and thus, not reliable in any way. Secondly, publicized data from studies represent the group that was studied within the frame of the study design, and therefore, cannot be automatically extrapolated to a general population, or to any individual patient. Thirdly, as stated before, even if there is a new treatment, that does not mean that it can be used in a particular case, since the drug might not be available for widely usage, the hospital where the patient is admitted might not carry it, the patient's insurance might not going to cover it, the treating physician might not feel comfortable in using something that is not widely accepted by the medical community and not recommended by medical societies and the FDA, yet, and the outcomes might be unknown at the current time. In other words, in many circumstances, likely there are no additional treatment options at a particular time available beyond what represents standard therapy at a given time.

To accept the limitations of medical therapy in many cases can be challenging for carrying family members, who in the vast majority of cases, do not have the baseline medical knowledge or the capacity to comprehend the medical situation but might look for answers or even for someone to blame for the current status quo of their loved ones. Exploring Google or other search engines on the web for a few hours does not replace or compare to years of attending medical school and decades of working in healthcare and does not make automatically everyone an expert in a field they might just have briefly read about on the web. I do not want to be misunderstood, I am all for a wider education and involvement of patients and family members in the care of their loved ones, which oftentimes requires additional information and gathering of data and exchange of thoughts and knowledge, but as physicians we are oftentimes preoccupied with medical language and not much understood by lay people. In addition, these kinds of conversations are very time consuming, and unfortunately, physicians do not have the luxury of spending much time per patient in view of economic limitations on one site while facing inhumane working hours on the other site.

Physicians are humans, too, and despite all available technologic sophistication, more often than not, have to realize and accept their limitations and helplessness in cases of incurable diseases and impending death. The physicians then have to cope also with the stress of disappointment, anger, death and grief. The physician's own spirituality, peace of mind, and faith might be helpful in coping with such situations. Unfortunately, there is hardly any lectures in medical school to prepare the physicians for this kind of stress and how to deal with it. Feeling of belonging to certain communities oftentimes might provide psychological, mental, and spiritual support, whether it is a family, a partnership, a neighborhood community, a sports club, or a church. Religion and faith in this sense appear more personal than all other traits or activities, and thus, might provide the individual with certain coping mechanisms and strengths - even in loneliness.

Accompanying dying patients in their final moments might make us accept God's will in Christianity, while we keep searching for ways to avoid or at least to delay death using medical and scientific research. As such we are at a crossroad where science meets faith, and many health care providers turn purely to science believing that faith should not be part of any medical management, while patients seem to welcome inquiries about their faith at chronic incurable illnesses or end-of life situations.

Data, facts, and theories in immortality research from a philosophical, theological and medical scientific aspect as well as the populistic ideas of everlasting life are critically evaluated, also in order to guide health care providers how to deal with their own faith and make them understand that religion and science are not competing but should be complementary in the holistic medical care of sick patients.

The goal of the present publication is to evaluate the current knowledge on human bodily immortality from a scientific and medical point of view as well as from a philosophical and theological approach. In particular, the religious view on immortality will be discussed based on the scriptures but also based on theology from different aspects.

The reason for this works is based on my own experiences as a physician dealing with patients' lives on a daily base. Healthcare providers who believe in Christian faith face certain ethical dilemmas at the current times:

1. There are enormous expectations from patients' and care givers' site to provide maximal care even in futile cases, in part based on the belief in populistic ideas of modern medicine providing biologic immortality.[1]

2. An increasing number of scientists are atheists proposing a case against religion since they believe that all life on earth and our entire existence can be reduced to incidental occurrences rather than by divine creation.[2]

3. Trust in advances in natural sciences oftentimes replaces religious faith and for many even might make Christian beliefs, doctrines and traditions obsolete.[3]

4. Biology can be explained as a computer software and thus, can be reprogrammed in its entirety.[4]

In order to provide answers to some but not all of the questions health care providers might have how to deal with conflicts of accepting death but hoping for immortality on earth or an existence after death we evaluate philosophical, theological as well as medical aspects of immortality.

1   Schwarz et al., "Maximal Care Considerations When Treating Patients with End-Stage Heart Failure," December 2011. moral, psychological and medico-legal challenge for health care providers. Especially in patients with chronic heart failure, the ethical and medico-legal issues associated with providing maximal possible care or withholding the same are coming to the forefront. Procedures, such as cardiac transplantation, have strict criteria for adequate candidacy. These criteria for subsequent listing are based on clinical outcome data but also reflect the reality of organ shortage. Lack of compliance and non-adherence to lifestyle changes represent relative contraindications to heart transplant candidacy. Mechanical circulatory support therapy using ventricular assist devices is becoming a more prominent therapeutic option for patients with end-stage heart failure who are not candidates for transplantation, which also requires strict criteria to enable beneficial outcome for the patient. Physicians need to critically reflect that in many cases, the patient's best interest might not always mean pursuing maximal technological options available. This article reflects on the multitude of critical issues that health care providers have to face while caring for patients with end-stage heart failure.","container-title":"Journal of Religion and Health","DOI":"10.1007/s10943-010-9326-y","ISSN":"1573-6571","issue":"4","journalAbbreviation":"J Relig Health","language":"eng","note":"PMID: 19191322\nPMCID: PMC3230758","page":"872-879","source":"PubMed","title":"Maximal care considerations when treating patients with end-stage heart failure: ethical and procedural quandaries in management of the very sick","title-short":"Maximal care considerations when treating patients with end-stage heart failure","volume":"50","author":[{"family":"Schwarz","given":"Ernst R."},{"family":"Philip","given":"Kiran J."},{"family":"Simsir","given":"Sinan A."},{"family":"Czer","given":"Lawrence"},{"family":"Trento","given":"Alfredo"},{"family":"Finder","given":"Stuart G."},{"family":"Cleenewerck","given":"Laurent A."}],"issued":{"date-parts":[["2011",12]]}}}],"schema":"https://github.com/citation-style-language/schema/raw/master/csl-citation.json"}

2   Keogh, "Theology After New Atheism."

3   Ryan, *Science and Spirituality*.

4   Kurzweil, *The Singularity Is Near*.

Chapter Two

Towards a Definition of "Immortality"

The first question is, why do humans have this enormous quest for immortality? It is something that has been there since centuries, to say the least, likely even longer since mankind is able to think. I believe that one of the main reasons why we all seek ways to live longer or even to think about living forever is our natural fear of death. This fear will affect almost everyone, sooner or later in life, usually not in early life but more frequently with advanced age, even though there is no maturity to learn a specific fear or an awareness of approaching death. The personal experience of someone dying in our close environment such as in our families, as an example, intensifies our thoughts and doubts and anxieties about what might be happening to us in an uncertain future. We are not mentally prepared instinctively for this incomprehensible future, but we are deeply troubled the moment we are seen someone close to us leaving this life. Even though it appears natural, we should consciously know that every single person in the world is going to die at one time and every single person who ever lived has either died or might be still alive but is going to die in the future, it is still a terrorizing thought to face death at one time. We are aware of the natural facts and the biologic laws of conception, birth, growth, aging, degeneration and death and the knowledge that these proceedings are completely outside of our own control – at least so we might think. But as the species we are, the most intelligent of all, the one that builds bridges, cities, rockets to reach the moon and artificial intelligence, there should be nothing impossible for us to investigate, manipulate and instigate, even life and death. Justin Martyr (100-165 AD), one of the early Christian apologists and philosophers believed that if a semen can build an entire human being, how can we believe that it might not be possible that we could live forever in a different sphere? Justin was not aware that it is not the semen alone but that an egg is required, too, but this does not change the idea that accepting the miracles of life opens our minds to acceptance and expectations - beyond our life. He further stated that "we expect to receive again our own bodies, though they be dead and cast into the earth, for we maintain that with God nothing is impossible".

On one hand, if we believe in God than we also believe in a life in Christ after our earthly death. On the other hand, as scientists and believers in the capabilities of the human mind, we must acknowledge the heroic advances in medicine and technology over the last one hundred years that overcame the plaque and tuberculosis and HIV and provided early treatments of heart attacks that all do prolong lives and save lives from death, at least at the moment. The century-old conflict between faith and science is obsolete and in a postmodern mind in our times in the twenty-first century beyond the rustiness of the Middle Ages and beyond the spiritual absence of enlightenment and the pessimism of Sartre and Nietzsche, one should not exclude the other, and vice versa.

Still, why the search for everlasting life? Why spending so much time, effort, and money on research on anti-aging and immortality? Do we forget that from the Pharaohs of Egypt to the Mayans and to the last centuries European Aristocrats, rulers and influential wealthy individuals spend all goods and wealth they had to fight diseases and death, but despite these efforts, nobody survived their own death at the end, anyhow? We might all be well aware of these facts but our consciousness and our rational knowledge does not prevent us from searching further, exploring, investigating, analyzing life, nature, diseases, and a way out, after all. This is – I guess - our God-given nature – at last.

According to the gospel of Thomas (Didymos Judas Thomas), Jesus said: *whoever finds the interpretation of these sayings will not taste death. As for the one who seeks, let him seek until he finds. When he finds he will become agitated, he will be astounded, and he will reign over the All.*

Or, as it is said in Romans 2:7: *To them who by persistence in doing good seek glory, honor and immortality, he will give eternal life.*

Therefore, even for Christians, the Holy Scripture makes it clear that man should seek, research, and even embrace the sciences with the aim for becoming immortal. Isn't that exactly what we as scientists (in medicine, technology, or theology) are trying to do?

Therefore, we might then ask ourselves: Is it wrong to aim for bodily immortality? Is it wrong in any ethical, moral, psychologic or philosophical-religious aspect to seek methods of anti-aging using modern technologies? Is aging so bad that we should try to fight it or is aging a natural process we should be proud of – as long as we can last to a point that one might call being at a *certain age?*

Instead, shouldn't we accept and praise the wonders of the circle of life rather than trying to defy nature? Is life as it is for the individual pre-determined so that – whatever we try to do, we have no influence whatsoever, anyhow? We still can die of an accident tomorrow, no matter how healthy we might eat, exercise, or how strong our physique might be. Many believe that thinks in life happen if there are meant to be, or they won't, if they are not meant to be. Is anything divinely determined? Do we have any say in what is going to happen to us tomorrow?

There are so many open questions that we might consider criticizing philosophically, but even if, it will not hinder us to move froward in our quest for immortality. One might even ask: is it sinful to ask for immortality? If one does a web search on this topic several questions come up such as: Is it a mortal sin for a Christian to seek immortality? Is human created immortality a sin? If bodily immortality was possible, would it be considered a sin, and why?

Even though some lay people as well as church people respond differently to this answer, I was somewhat baffled by one of the answers someone gave:

"It is probably (a sin) as you are at least committing three of the seven cardinal (deadly) sins which are Christian-based belief: gluttony – wanting excessive consumption in life, greed - wanting excessive power and wealth, pride - thinking you are better than others, envy - wanting your Christian Gods supernatural powers".

As a Christian, a natural scientist and a physician, I completely disagree with this idea. Just the opposite, I strongly believe that it is our task to pro-long life, to save life, to limit suffering by fighting diseases, and to alleviate the miseries that accompany advanced age, immobility, and weakness, for all humankind. In my opinion, the quest for immortality is not a pursuit for creating a novel transhuman computer combined with the human species but to prolong life within our existence. On one hand this mission is Catho-lic in its traditional Christian Churches' view as well as in its original sense of the term, i.e., universal, ecumenic, spiritual, interfaith/interreligious, but in a sense it even can be seen as atheistic/irreligious, agnostic, and blasphemous on the other hand.

Is immortality of the soul what Christianity has in mind? It appears much easier to believe in the philosophical traditions of an immortality of the soul alone, a continued existence of an immaterial soul, a mind or a human spirit after the physical death of the material body. It is easier com-prehensible because we know how the material body, the corpse, will decay after death, until nothing is left but atoms or chemical molecules that might feed into the life cycle of other structures and the earth after our death. We cannot see and explain the soul very well but we can see and understand the body. What we cannot see, we can believe in. But if we see the lifeless corpse of a person who was alive before, we cannot easily imagine how a corpse like this could be re-vitalized into a living person in this world.

According to Christian faith, the resurrection is conceived as an indis-soluble psycho-physical unity rather than a ghostly or mental entity flying around in the sky. But the immortal soul that goes back to Plato is not a Christian doctrine ad ipso. There is no mention of any immortal soul anywhere in the biblical scriptures. In fact, as we will discuss later, in Christianity, the resurrection is not the soul alone but the re-embodiment of the soul, meaning the re-vitalization of the whole individual including his/her earthly bodily matter.

Besides the religious ideas and the faith in resurrection and everlasting life, the next more popular question might be if the dream of everlasting life (or everlasting youth) even is becoming a hypothetical reality during our lifetime? If you watch TV and listen to the concepts of futurists it seems that these ideas are much further investigated than we did imagine a few years ago, and the results appear promising enough to expect a major change during our lifespan and our health span over the next decade or so.

The quest for immortality from a theological perspective lets us dive deeply into the biblical meaning of death, the Alchemy with its search for the Philosopher's Stone and elixirs for the fountain of youth, and the eschatological evaluation of human existence and the destiny at the end including immortality of the immaterial soul.

The medical perspective shows us the current efforts and successes of life extension and research efforts on anti-aging and regenerative medicine as well the biological basis to overcome the Hayflick limit (the cessation of cellular division).[5]

We then need to review and critically evaluate the disputes whether the medical sciences and Christian beliefs are in strict contrast to each other. We will explore, however, that this in fact is not the case.

---

5   Shay and Wright, "Hayflick, His Limit, and Cellular Ageing."

Chapter Three

Medicine and Immortality

Medicine and immortality are two terms that - in theory - have nothing to do with each other. Medicine is the science of helping the diseased, curing illnesses, and mainly alleviating symptoms. We can summarize the causes for any illnesses or disease related symptoms as a result of one of the following twelve conditions which epitomize more than 90% of all health disorders:

1. traumatic injury,
2. reactive inflammation,
3. acute infection,
4. blood clotting or bleeding issues
5. vascular compromise (including blood vessel occlusions),
6. malignant mutation,
7. pregnancy (even though this is not considered a disease),
8. toxins,
9. allergic or immunologic reactions,
10. mental disorders,
11. congenital defects,
12. wear and tear degeneration.

As physicians, we practice medicine when patients come to our clinics, to urgent care facilities or to the hospitals because they might feel unwell, or experience pain, or they suffer from loss of function. Doctors then try to establish a diagnosis that could explain the current problem, based on their personal training and education, their knowledge and experience, and commonly accepted guideline recommendations from professional societies using their senses such as their eyes, ears, hands, and stethoscopes, before ordering further testing such as imaging and laboratory modalities to verify their initial working hypothesis. At the same time, they initiate treatment of symptoms to improve the condition of the patient and to alleviate suffering, and once further diagnostics have established underlying causes, then additional treatment is initiated to manage the causal condition and prevent further harm.

Always, the first goal of any treatment is symptom- and pain relief, followed by avoidance of further harm to organs, and subsequently to regain functionality of the entire organism, restitution to a functional state, and prevention of degeneration and premature death.

Doing so, health care providers actually *do* prolong life in many cases all the time.

As a cardiologist, almost every single day I do encounter patients with acute heart attacks and then I take them to the cardiac catheterization laboratory in order to open clogged arteries to alleviate chest pain, salvage ischemic heart tissue from becoming necrotic, and to prevent death in the acute setting, but also to protect heart muscle cells and organ function and patient's lives in the mid- and long-term run.[6]

Symptom relief and prevention of damage, inhibition of loss of function and fighting against death are the main pillars of practicing medicine. Even though technology has advanced, this original dogma of clinical and practical medicine has not changed over thousands of years.[7]

As with many other sciences, medicine has evolved and has also created subspecialities and different branches that are somewhat related to the original science, but quite different, such as alchemy. Alchemy, in contrast to

---

6   EISDORFER, "ON THE PROLONGATION OF LIFE."
7   Ledermann, "Dogmas Of Medicine."

medicine, is the medieval chemical science and philosophy aiming to achieve the transmutation of the base metals into gold, the discovery of a universal cure for disease, and the discovery of a means of indefinitely prolonging life.[8] Alchemists in their traditional "medical" profession attempted to create human immortality.

In recent years more than ever before, the scientific processes of aging have been more extensively investigated, in particular in connection with the development of the concept of regenerative medicine using stem cell research.[9] The concept is to switch from the traditional *reactive medicine* to *regenerative or reparative medicine*. Using the pluripotency of stem cells that can build entire organs developed into the idea of administering stem cells into diseased organisms with the goal to re-build damaged tissue and repair injury to re-establish a fully functional and healthy state.[10] This concept has become popular not only among scientists but even more among the public that enabled a non-scientific market of stem cell clinics promising cure of diseases and rejuvenation by stem cell injections - for cash. Even though stem cells do work, many of these establishments do lack the academic and clinical reputation but obviously have good marketing strategies to create a business out of it. In its extreme forms, I personally have encountered wealthy individuals who became obsessed with the stem cell concept.

I remember Mr. N., a 70year old billionaire who saw his own mother dying of an incurable lung disease and was terrified by the idea that he might end up in a similar condition in just a few years. His idea was that "if we cannot take anything with us *(when we die)*, then we should not leave" (original citation). In other words, this individual spent a lot of money to "re-create myself in a Petry dish before I was born" (Chris Hansen Report 2021, CNN report 2016) using somatic cell transfer technology that is illegal in most countries and unethical using embryonic cellular material, in order to create his own immortality. Besides the questionable psychopathology of this individual, it demonstrates an exaggerated obsession for bodily immortality, which most likely neither him nor anyone else will achieve in our lifetime.

---

8   Straus, "Alchemy."
9   Edgar et al., "Regenerative Medicine, Organ Bioengineering and Transplantation."
10   Schwarz, *The Secret World of Stem Cell Therapy.*

Chapter Four

What is Immortality?

Before trying to overcome mortality and create immortality, let us establish a few concepts first about definitions and facts. What is immortality?

Immortality is the opposite of mortality. Mortality is defined as the state being subject to death or destined to die. Mortality is also impermanence or temporality. Mortality in medicine defines the rate or state of death or the number of deaths among a certain group of patients, according to the National Cancer Institute. As such, mortality refers to the number of deaths within a distinct population and within a distinct period of time. The mortality of certain forms of diseases describes its risk of dying from it, usually as a function of time. As an example, the 5-year mortality rate of stage IV breast cancer is 73%, which means that the 5-year survival rate is 27%. [11] In this context, survival is considered to be the opposite of mortality.

Immortality, on the other hand, is the reverse of mortality but not in a medical sciences context.

Survival is not immortality since it is limited in time and only represents the continuation of existence at one point in time.

---

11   Torre et al., "Global Cancer Incidence and Mortality Rates and Trends--An Update."

Longevity represents the likelihood of survival for a period of time.

Immortality represents the continuation of a living existence without an end – meaning forever.

Until now, in contrast to survival and longevity, the term *immortality* does not really exist in a practical medical vocabulary.

Immortality in a natural scientific context means the never-ending existence of species that are undergoing adaptive mechanisms in order to deal with different living conditions and have the ability to regenerate endlessly. In this context, biology scientists have discovered certain species that do live for a prolonged period of time and are considered "immortal" in a scientific sense, which means they do not die of aging or age-related alterations - but they still might die physically by trauma or predators.

Today, the only species that is considered physically immortal at this time is a jelly fish, named Turritopsis doohmii. [12]

The jellyfish returns to its polyp stage over a three-day period in case of any injury or disease, transforming its cells into a younger state that will eventually grow into adulthood all over again.

Certain bacteriae such as the Deinococcus radiodurans, have DNA repair mechanisms in place that makes them live forever, even if exposed to extreme temperatures or even radiation (as the given name suggests), therefore they are classified as poly-extremophilic.[13]

Also, planarian worms are known for their regeneration abilities. If the worm is cut in the middle, both portions can live independently and grow to a full-sized worm. They also repair age-related or disease-related damage, thereby living for a prolonged period of time, if not forever.

Lobsters and turtles have been shown to hardly age if at all, and usually die of illnesses rather than of aging. Certain turtles can live for several centuries.

Similarly, some whales showed injuries from weapons that were used in the early 1800s, and the oldest bowhead whale was supposed to be 211

---

12   Devarapalli et al., "The Conserved Mitochondrial Gene Distribution in Relatives of Turritopsis Nutricula, an Immortal Jellyfish."defining itself as the only immortal organism in the animal kingdom. Therefore, the animal is having prime importance in basic biological, aging, and biomedical researches. However, till date, the genome of this organism has not been sequenced and even there is no molecular phylogenetic study to reveal its close relatives. Here, using phylogenetic analysis based on available 16s rRNA gene and protein sequences of Cytochrome oxidase subunit-I (COI or COX1

13   Wang et al., "Gene Regulation for the Extreme Resistance to Ionizing Radiation of Deinococcus Radiodurans."

years old. More recently, a Greenland shark was detected that - according to marine scientists - was over 400 years old.[14] Of note, these sharks have an enormous amount of stem cells that constantly regenerate their teeth (and obviously they swim a lot and eat a lot of fish, which might not be a bad thing with regard to a long life).

These are a few examples for an enormous regenerative ability by DNA repair mechanisms and stem cells that can develop into any tissue type and are responsible for survival, longevity, and maybe - physical immortality. [15]

It is not quite clear whether it is really immortality on man's mind to wish for or whether it is more the search for prevention of aging and age-related conditions, diseases, and loss of function. It is apparently more eternal youth and vitality (the fountain of youth) man seeks rather than immortality. Age itself is the strongest risk factor for dying, and age is also the number one reason for disease and death, and the number one predictor of death. On average, every day approximately 100,000 people die as a result of aging. [16]

Preventing aging, however, is not similar with immortality. Medicine in today's world, mainly deals with sick-care rather than with healthcare, especially by dealing with age-related changes in health, whether it is vascular atherosclerosis, heart diseases and strokes, cancer or chronic degenerative changes, that not only limit our lifespan but in particular does diminish substantially our quality of life.[17]

The *anti-aging* movement in medicine attempts to prevent the development of age-related illnesses but in large parts, lacks appropriate scientific background. [18] At its best, these efforts might help to delay the progression of chronic degenerative diseases. In this sense, anti-aging is different from immortality. And immortality in a physical sense does not mean invincibility.

To delay or prevent aging we must counteract the processes of senescence (biological aging). [19] The researchers who are trying to do so are often-

---

14   "400-Year-Old Greenland Shark 'Longest-Living Vertebrate.'"
15   Stenvinkel and Shiels, "Long-Lived Animals with Negligible Senescence."
16   ThriftBooks, "Ending Aging."
17   Comhaire and Decleer, "Can the Biological Mechanisms of Ageing Be Corrected by Food Supplementation. The Concept of Health Care over Sick Care."
18   Gorzoni and Pires, "[Is there any scientific evidence supporting antiaging medicine?"
19   Herranz and Gil, "Mechanisms and Functions of Cellular Senescence."

times called healthspanners since they attempt to extend lifespan (and health span), whereas those who seek immortality are referred to as immortalists.[20]

In contrast, immortality in a theologic sense means everlasting or eternal life after death, in Christianity as a result of the resurrection, in a sphere beyond our human comprehension, which is a divine concept for believers of the faith if not for all human beings.

As we will establish more detailed later, there is not just one form of immortality.

---

20   Rachello and O'Connell, "Lives of the Immortalists."

Chapter Five

Problems with Immortality

H
ealth care providers face bioethical dilemmas regarding maximal care considerations in dying patients believing in and fighting for biologic immortality but also as scientists, to defend religious beliefs against an atheistic science-driven movement against all forms of religion. Especially for Christians working in health care, it is important to understand that religion does accept science and science does neither negate faith nor does it not make faith obsolete.

Immortality is a quest of human nature. Of interest, this quest starts in early adulthood and appears be of greater importance with increasing age. Children usually do not have such a quest since their world is preoccupied with present play and care for them. Adolescents usually are so occupied in life and dreams of adulthood, relationships, education and careers that leaves little room for thoughts about what comes thereafter, whereas adults with more life experience and the familiarity of losing family members, especially their parents or friends, might have faced consequences of death in their close environment. In view of progression of aging and the development of chronic diseases as well as a decline of functionality and awareness of bodily degeneration as a result of aging, however, the human fear of a steadily and progressive decline resulting in final death becomes much more prominent on one's mind. Therefore, the question about what is happening thereafter becomes a major interest for the human mind. This interest is mainly driven by fear of the unknown. All religions offer to some degree the option of an afterlife or eternal life, and philosophy dating back to Plato considers the existence of an immortal soul that cannot be destroyed and is in existence after our bodily death. The Scriptures, the Old Testament, does not mention an immortal soul, and for Judaism, death itself, is final. From a Christian point of view, the soul is life and gives life but cannot exist without a body. Christianity therefore teaches the resurrection, i.e., the rebirth after death as evidenced by the resurrection of Jesus Christ after his crucifixion and resulting death. [21]

Science in general and medical science in particular aims at reducing suffering, treating diseases, and improving survival of diseases. Medicine in its traditional but most commonly used version up until today is reactive, i.e., physicians react to the phenomena of diseases. Patients come to medical practices or hospitals because of symptoms of a disease or loss of a function of an organ as a consequence of a disease. The reaction of practical medicine then attempts to treat these symptoms, relieve suffering, avoid further harm, and improve functionality. As a side effect of such treatment but not as the primary goal initially, survival can be achieved, and life-span can be extended.

Modern medicine, however, now attempts to make a paradigm shift from reactive to regenerative medicine. [22] Instead of dealing with the consequences of damage, regenerative medicine attempts to repair damage, and by thus, restore functionality to the status quo prior to the disease. Furthermore, the idea of regeneration expands towards prevention of disease and even to mechanisms of "anti-aging". While anti-aging is not really a scientific term, the movement of anti-aging management targets all age-related diseases (which is most of the diseases anyhow) by applying regenerative powers, for example in the form of stem cell therapy. Some believe that stem cell therapy by means of regeneration might be able to represent the fountain of youth

21   Church, *Catechism of the Catholic Church.*
22   Schwarz, *The Secret World of Stem Cell Therapy.*

and possibly, the path to immortality. While anti-aging medicine including regenerative medicine likely might be able to expand health-span, it also might expand life-span. The scientific context of extending life, however, is in strict contrast to the philosophical and religious idea of immortality of the individual. The gap between scientific technology of prolonging life and the religious faith on immortality are evaluated in a systematic manner based on published data.

Our research explores and evaluates the hypothesis that the medical quest for physical immortality is largely compatible with religious tenets, provided that certain parameters of intentionality and bioethics are respected, which is in particular of interests for health care providers facing challenges of high tech medical care for patients with incurable end-stage diseases requesting everything to be done to prolong life while also facing issues of conflicts between personal faith and scientific advances.

The aim of my writings is to demonstrate that advances in medicine and biotechnology towards prolongation of life on earth is not contradicting Christian faith.

Furthermore, I attempt to proof that the Catholic Church does not oppose advances in sciences based on Sacred Scripture and the writings of Catholic theologians from antique to the Middle Ages to the 21st century.

Chapter Six

Theology and Medicine

Christian faith does not contradict any progress in biotechnology to prolong life in medicine, and science on immortality does not replace faith in God as the creator of all being. Especially for health care providers, a symbiosis rather than a conflict between religion and science is essential for their own spiritual health and also for their work in perspective of bioethical decision making for end-of life care.

Historically, theology has been considered the "supreme science", especially in the Middle Ages in European academic institutions and universities, which included the study of God, the Scriptures, history, rhetoric, knowledge, and philosophy. In the 20th century, however, this supremacy was taken over by medical and biophysical sciences ("Naturwissenschaften" in German universities) that deal with a very systematic approach to replicate and explain natural processes by use of controlled experiments and analysis, especially in physics, chemistry, and biology.

Theology, religion and faith were then considered contrasting any scientific explanation - and vice versa. The beginning of humankind in Genesis in the Old Testament where man (Adam) was made out of the dust of the earth and the woman (Eve) was made from the rib of man is in contrast to evolutionary theories in science examining the development from simple

23

single cellular species to multicellular organisms to different animals and then to higher brain capacity species such as monkeys and lastly the neandertals among other first human beings. The 'new (natural) science' is in part contradicting the 'old (theological) science', and the pre-eminence of biophysics and technology has taken over the faith in religion, by many.

Accordingly, but not surprisingly, the humans' quest for bodily immortality nowadays is one of the predominant targets of natural sciences and technology rather than of faith in religious doctrines alone.

The gap between the possibilities of modern technologies achieving longer lasting life and the philosophical and religious ideas of human immortality is getting closer than ever in history, mainly based on the opportunities provided by advanced medical therapies including regenerative medicine.

Since the beginning of human life in time - as far as we know – mankind has an emotional and perhaps irrational attachment to our bodies that creates the quest for ever-lasting youth, perfect health, and immortality. Many philosophies consider an immortal soul after death as also proposed by Plato. Every religion offers existence beyond the *here and now* on earth after our bodily demise. The three great monotheistic religions Judaism, Christianity and Islam believe and teach that immortality is achieved through the resurrection of the body together with the soul at the time of the final judgement.

We are revealing some religious but mainly the Christian ideas of immortality in brief without claiming to be all inclusive, and we also demonstrate that the achievements and advances of modern medicine do provide the opportunity for increased health span, survival of certain diseases that were deadly in the past, and prolongation of life including maintained functionality and quality of life at high ages. Medicine, however, does not provide immortality and does not interfere with the Christian or any religious faith of everlasting life. Therefore, medicine which is considered the queen of the predominant natural sciences, does not replace the Christian quest to live a righteous life and the faith in the resurrection of the body to gain immortality.

Chapter Seven

Literature Review on Immortality

I n order to get a better idea about immortality from a philosophical, biological and theological approach, a literature search was conducted on the topic. Even though a search on such as huge topic can never be complete, it was attempted to focus on the following issues:

For biology and medicine, we focused on current research especially using Pubmed on anti-aging and immortality where it to refers to a possible meaning for the human being with regard to advances in modern medicine. As search parameters and keywords we focused on *immortality, anti-aging, prolongation of life, cell death, senescence, aging, biotechnology,* mostly in combination, as well as clinical study data on the topic. We did not include cellular or cell culture studies, and we omitted specifics on certain medications that might affect cellular death such as chemotherapeutic agents that might affect cellular division or antiviral medications that might affect cellular survival in any way. Case reports were excluded, only articles written in English and German were included.

For philosophy and theology, the search terms immortality, ever-lasting life, eternal life, mortality, survival, theology, Roman Catholic theology, religion, faith, reason, and philosophy were used, mostly in combination, using JSTOR. In addition, Google searches were conducted on specific terms such as *Rahner and eternal life, Ratzinger and eschatology, theology and immortality,* as examples. Only published scientific articles and books and book chapters were included, as well as (rarely) published press articles if no other publications on the topic were available (such as the *Pope's statement on evolution,* as an example). With very few exceptions, reports based on website write-ups were not included, unless these provided information not available elsewhere (such as the scientific conferences organized by the Pontifical Academy of Sciences on www.pas.va).

For the populistic view on immortality, internet searches were conducted based on references in published books such as a search on the futurist *Ray Kurzweil* based on his appearance in *Immortality, Inc.* by Chip Walter. Similarly, none of these searches were meant to be all inclusive but rather focused on current popular issues surrounding the belief in immortality.

Currently, there is a huge discrepancy between religions and the natural sciences with regard to views on immortality. [23] The faith (in any religion) in ever-lasting life, immortality of the soul or the body and the soul, or the resurrection (coming back to life after death) is a personal choice that is encouraged and taught by the Churches and religious communities. Immortality in this sense is usually a life of the individual beyond the earthly existence, whether it is in heaven, hell, or Nirvana or in any sphere beyond our human knowledge and imagination. [24,25,26] Immortality in this sense cannot be explained by any scientific means and cannot be reproduced in a research laboratory. Scientific advances in modern biotechnology on the other hand, have now taught us to understand the biologic and pathophysiologic processes of senescence (cellular aging). Our group previously has evaluated the different versions of cellular death such as necrosis, apoptosis, and autophagic cell death. [27,28] Moreover, the manipulation of genetically pre-determined mechanisms by use of genetic DNA reprogramming to avoid cellular aging and death [29] as well as repair possibilities utilizing regenerative methods to

23   Ecklund et al., "Religion among Scientists in International Context."
24   Hynson, "Religion, Attendance, and Belief in an Afterlife."
25   Hawkins, "Lost and Found."
26   Ghayas and Batool, "Construction and Validation of Afterlife Belief Scale for Muslims."
27   Kunapuli, Rosanio, and Schwarz, ""How Do Cardiomyocytes Die?"
28   Elmore, "Apoptosis."
29   Rando and Chang, "Aging, Rejuvenation, and Epigenetic Reprogramming."

replace damage tissues using stem cell therapy [30] now offers the scientific opportunities to prolong life and overcome consequences of certain disease in theory, in the research laboratory, and obviously in clinical practice, too. [31]

As a result of this discrepancy, religion and faith remain independent on any advances in sciences and biotechnology for the individual and the religious or spiritual community. Biotechnology on the other hand, does not need any religion or personal faith to move forward.

This accumulates in an ethical dilemma for the individual but also for health care providers because of the continuous quest for immortality among all cultures and religions.

Because of the above, from a physician's point of view, there are two issues to deal with: 1. It is becoming more difficult to deal with patients' requests and expectations in view of currently available medicine in contrast to the media hype on possible future treatments; 2. Technology and science should never replace the individuals' faith and beliefs in a higher power which should be respected, while faith should not stand in the way of scientific progress, either.

30   Kwon et al., "Recent Advances in Stem Cell Therapeutics and Tissue Engineering Strategies."
31   Schwarz, *The Secret World of Stem Cell Therapy.*

Chapter Eight

Life

Before we dive into the ideas of mortality, immortality and death, we might need to review life as it is and as it is meant to be. Life is existence. Life means active interaction of a living organisms with its environment. To be interactive, the being has to be alive. It has to have biologic activity of metabolism and growth and demise. It also has to have consciousness – or a soul in a Thomistic sense (a plant has a plant soul, an animal has an animal soul)[32]. Life is the opposite of death.

While things are composed of form and matter, so is Life. But form and matter can be a chair, which matter is composed of wood, but the hand-crafted design makes the wood into a chair which then represent its form and serves its function, according to Thomas Aquinas. There might be entities without matter but just form, for example angels. If angels exist, they are supposed to be bodyless, so they have not matter, but a form. Life has to have both, form and matter. But form and matter alone does not make anything alive, but soul does. The soul, again according to Aquinus, is the spirit, the energy that makes a living being. A palm tree is alive and has a plant soul, an animal is alive and has an animal soul, and a human has a human soul,

---

32   Aquinas, *The Summa Theologica of St. Thomas Aquinas*.

whereas a computer or car are machines without a soul, and therefore are not considered living things.

The pure form as well as the soul, both may be beyond natural sciences comprehension and *explainability* (is this even a word – but if not, I am sure the reader gets the point). A thing with form but no matter, should not be alive. A thing without a soul, is also not a living creature. So, if angels exist, are they not alive? They could be, theoretically, since they have a form, but no matter. Thoughts can have a form, but no matter, therefore they are not considered living entities. Therefore all living things likely have to have a form, a matter (maybe except angels), and a soul to be alive.

What is the soul? The philosophical and theological ideas of the soul go way beyond our understanding of biology. As far as we know, life always consists of form and matter, but again, that alone would not make anything alive. It requires much more than that. It has to have energy and self-activity, meaning not controlled, fed or programmed by an outside source (like a battery that feeds a cellphone that uses SIRI to talk to us). Life represents the essence of biology in contrast to inorganic matter, and life by definition is 'in-time", meaning it is subject to undergoing changes and thus, is limited. There is no existence after life. Life is also characterized by the ability to get and to use energy and to adapt and response to change. Most importantly, however, appears the fact that life – in contrast to everything not being alive – is reproducing and thus, capable of creating life, a characteristic which loses its efficacy secondary to biologic degeneration over time. Human life starts at fertilization with the embryo's conception, the formation of the zygote which is a diploid cell resulting from the fusion of two haploid gametes representing the female derived egg fertilized by a male sperm initiated the human development. The zygote already contains all the genetic information from the father's sperm and the mother's ovum to build an entire organism and human being. The cellular divisions, growth and development then form an embryo, which his defined as the early stages of a multicellular organism. The embryonic stage is followed by a fetus, which is the term used from week 11 during pregnancy. An embryo is not considered a person, but a late state fetus is a person, a fact that has implications for abortion legalities. There have been discussions among people of faith and scientists and the lay public about when life starts. Some argue that according to Genesis 2:7, life begins with the first breath. However, it appears obvious that a baby on the mother womb that is interacting, growing, kicking, and moving around is definitely alive. Therefore, long before birth, the human embryo growing in utero is a living being. In Catholicism, the embryo is considered a complete human being, a person, which is the base for its dogma on the conservation of life and strict rejection of abortion at any time, as outlined by Pope Benedict XVI words in 2005: "the loving eyes of God look onto the human being, considered full and complete at its beginning" by interpreting Psalm 139 ("thou didst see my limbs unformed in the womb, and in thy book they are all recorded").

Besides human life, animals and plants are living organisms, so are worms or bacteriae. Fungal spores which are dormant cells surviving extreme conditions for prolonged periods of time, are considered a living thing, even though there might be different opinions. What about viruses? Are viruses that can replicate and interact living beings? Even though there are different opinions about the correct answer, fact is that viruses represent a gray area between living organisms and non-living particles, since they require host cells to replicate, and in a host environment. Viruses definitely can manipulate and alter these cells and even entire tissues, and they can take over control, and even kill (as profoundly seen recently with the COVID-19 pandemic worldwide). In my opinion, for the above reasons, viruses are not considered living entities but particles that can affect living cells and use those to fuel their desire and destination.

Why is this distinction even important? It might become important if we consider biologic research on simple organisms on immortality to decide whether or not we are dealing with living structures or just particles that are used by living cells or vice versa. If these are not living structures, then study results might not be easily extrapolated to living entities such as cells or entire organisms. On the other hand, studies in living structures can provide insights into cellular processes of aging and its genetic DNA composition that determines senescence. In this context, I just came across a Youtube video a few days ago that demonstrated a worm that was cut into three pieces, and in a timely manner, all three pieces from the original living single worm were able to grow and replace the cut-off portions and to continue to live on as three separate worms. The reason for this enormous capability of regenerative power – at least in part – is based on the fact that these worms have an abundance of stem cells that are able to regenerate damaged or removed tissues in their totality.

The goals of any life are: 1) to live, 2) to survive, 3) to reproduce 4) to live in happiness.

Out of those (among other goals,) the most important is to live and to survive, which instinctively is engrafted into our DNA. This instinct is a protective mechanism that also creates defense, fear, fight and flight responses. We are born with the intuitive fear and retrieval upon strange encounters, but our own protection is not developed to defend ourselves until we almost reach adult size. All our natural instincts are based on survival, whether it is to create hunger and thirst, and protection or shelter in case of outside predator attacks. Of interest, several mechanisms can interfere with these inert protective mechanisms such as drugs, disease, toxins, alcohol among others. Furthermore, with cerebral degeneration with increased age such as dementia, we also lose some of these protective mechanisms, which might represent some kind of (social and societal) Darwinism, i.e., survival of the fittest and strongest – only.

Reproduction on the other hand, is age dependent, meaning there is life but without reproductive properties at young ages or at old ages, therefore reproduction is not a prerequisite for being alive. Failure to reproduce, however, therefore might represent either a stage of early development in childhood which has no reproductive powers, or a stage of degeneration of productive organs (in women earlier than in men) at advanced ages. Reproduction, therefore, even though a pre-requisite for becoming alive (since we all stem from a single egg cell and a sperm cell), is not a prerequisite for being alive.

Scholars as well as lay people have asked themselves since at least centuries if not since the very beginning what is the purpose of life, what is the reason why we exist on earth, and why are we who we are. It is beyond normal understanding to get a grip on the reasons why, and what the ultimate goal for our human existence might be. Moreover, it is mysterious what our individual purpose should be in life, and more or less, we all try to figure that out, don't we? Despite the secularization of the modern technological materialistic world where religion and faith and spirituality has rather any place in most peoples' lives, we all have thoughts of the purpose, which then often translates into personalized dreams and goals of pecuniary value rather than of existentialism. The goals are predetermined by our upbringing, in which adherence to societal and governmental normative regulations is more important than the nurturing of anyone's creative proficiencies. We are forced and learn to go to school, get an education and try to make money to buy a house and a nice car and spent nice vacations in beautiful locations for a short period of the year in summertime. The ultimate goal for all our daily efforts studying or working ultimately is, happiness. This kind of happiness then is oftentimes mistakenly declared as monetary wealth and independence, professional power, and public acceptance. The facts are obvious that these attributes do not provide pure happiness, if so, the rich and powerful would be always happy and there would be no crime or suicide or drug addictions among then. We all know that reality proves the farthest of these fantastic principles. For most however, once the ideas of money and leading positions have not come true as anticipated, the little things in life might become more important, such as watching grandkids play or enjoying the silence of a soulmate's understanding or watching flowers growing in spring and birds chirping in a summer morning.

Many Christians believe that the purpose of human's creation is the do good and to look after whatever God has created (our world) in a kind of stewardship. Doing good in this sense means to follow God's creation and Jesus Christ's words and mission by helping others, being justice, not doing any harm and providing to the needed, in order to receive the earnings in the form of a divine salvation at the end of our lives.

Live obviously is still a mystery, since despite evolutionary explanations of the *how* of the beginning of life, the *why* remains unknown, and thus, belongs to the incomprehensibility of the creator God.

Before life, there is no existence. After life, what is there?

Chapter Nine

Life Expectancy and Immortality

L ife expectancy for human beings has drastically changed over the last centuries, and likely is going to change further in the very near future. Even biologic life prolongation or some kind of immortality as per our understanding seems to be within scientific reach in the not too far future and might be created in the experimental setting using cell cultures or animal models, this does not automatically translate into a broad life extension for all mankind, yet.

The average life expectancy during the Bronze Age (approximately 3000 until 300 B.C.) was 26 years of age and has not much changed for 2000 years: in the early 1900, the worlds average life expectancy was 30 years, in 1950 it was 48, and in 2017 it was 72 years of age. The main determinants for life expectancy are childbirth rates, death secondary to infection especially in times of pandemics, and in adulthood, especially the impact of cardiovascular diseases.

According to these numbers, change in life expectancy is more caused by a reduction in early death rather than by a true life extension. Of interest, according to the Scriptures in the Old Testament, people in the B.C. era lived much longer than today (i.e., hundreds of years, Enoch even had children at his age above 300 years), and the oldest man in the Scriptures became

969 years old (Methuselah). After the flood when God created the Noahic Covenant, however, human life expectancy was decreased to less than 120 years. One biblical explanation for this drastic reduction in life expectancy was that less years would translate into less chances to commit sins. Many theological scholars have argued whether or not these ages in years were really comparable to our modern years according to the Gregorian calendar. Before the flood, the average age of man in Genesis is 912 years: Enosh lived 905 years, Cainan 910, Jared 962, and Methuselah 965 years. Even after the flood, people lived long, for example Abraham became 175 years of age, Moses 120 years, Jacob 147 years, and Isaac 180 years, to name a few.

Again, from a medical point of view with regard to our current understanding, it seems almost impossible to believe that someone could have lived up to even 150 years - in the absence of modern medicine. Scientifically, however, it is not impossible.

Biblical scholars have argued whether these years are in fact years of the individual, or cumulative years of the individual clan or family tribes. Others state that numbers are not to be taken literal but numerologically, meaning symbolic.[33] In addition, some authors played with numbers since only 0, 2, 5, 7 and 9 occurred in biblical writings, arguing all of the numbers can be expressed as combinations of the two "sacred" numbers 60 and 7 in terms of years and months, which apparently is not explained randomly. Others think that biblical age numbers are purely symbols or might representing epochs or dynasties.[34]

Most biblical exegetics argue, however, that it is actually the individuals' ages mentioned here and not their tribes' ages, because of healthier dietary habits and the earths radiation protection before the flood.

From an analytical point of view, the biblical writings with regard to many topics in Genesis including men's ages, might rather need to be understood symbolically. However, the Catholic Church has not officially commented on that issue of the mentioned ages of men before the flood.

---

33   "Long Life Spans in Genesis."
34   "Did Methuselah Really Live 969 Years?"

In any case, life expectancy has significantly increased over the last century compared to any period within the last 2000 years or even before, secondary to advance sin modern medicine and health care including reduction in newborn deaths, use of antibiotics and vaccinations, and improvements in the treatment of injuries and cardiovascular diseases. The highest life expectancy at the current time have women in Japan with more than 84 years, followed by the industrialized nations in the Western world with mid 70s-80 years of age, whereas life expectancy in developing nations is significantly lower.

Chapter Ten

Death

Before evaluating immortality and its impact on life and nature, we should first elaborate on life and nature and its biologic course, which is death. Death by definition, is the irreversible cessation of all bodily function, or the permanent ending of vital processes in body, tissues and cells. As such, death is the end of life and the definite end of existence of a person or an organism.

Death is therefore the non-existence of someone or something that has lived before. Death is the absolute nothing. Death in this sense could be seen similar to the status before birth or better, before conception, which also is non-existence. Death also is part of the natural course of life, which start with conception, then leads to growth, followed by degeneration, and ends with dying.

Death can occur at any moment for a cell or any living being, it can be abrupt, unexpected, or it can be the result of a slower cessation of biologic processes. The abrupt form can be caused by an outside event such as an accident or trauma, or ingestion of toxic substances, or a sudden internal event such an arrhythmia (sudden cardiac death), a heart attack, stroke, pulmonary embolism, a brain bleeding caused by a ruptured aneurysm, among many other reasons, whereas the slow process usually is considered a result of degeneration and aging leading to irreversible organ failure, which can be caused by age itself, or by lack of oxygen, cancers, or progressive organ specific failures. At the end, it is always cardiac arrest which defines the time of death since the heart stops at one time, and with that, there is no more circulation within the body.

In death, we must consider medical, legal, ethical cultural, religious, philosophical, and societal issues that might be of relevance for the person who died but also for the families, care givers, friends, communities and societies.

Medically, we must distinguish the different terminology that defines death of a person, also for medical-legal reasons. California Law, as an example, has Article 1, the Uniform Determination of Death Act which states that a) *an individual who has sustained either (1) irreversible cessation of circulatory and respiratory functions, or (2) irreversible cessation of all functions of the entire brain, including the brain stem, is dead. A determination of death must be made in accordance with accepted medical standards.*

Irreversible cessation of all brain functions, therefore, is considered brain death. Medically, death is defined also as the irreversible loss of the capacity for consciousness, combined with the irreversible loss of the capacity to breathe. However, as the reader can easily understand, there can be situations in which a patient might not regain consciousness (ever) as a result of irreversible brain damage but with some degree of maintained brain stem function (as a result of a massive stroke or carbon monoxide poisoning among other causes) without the ability of spontaneous breathing, but the body is kept alive through the use of ventilators providing oxygenation to the lungs and the heart, and the whole body. Such a vegetative state is usually irreversible, but does not represent death, until cessation of respirator therapy might then lead to hypoxia and cardiac arrest leading to death. There are other cases of vegetative states where individuals have lived for many years or even decades without regaining consciousness but with maintained respiratory function and cardiac function, such as the case of Terri Schiavo in Florida in 2005.[35]

For transplant medicine, the definition of brain death is of essence which is required prior to any organ use for transplantation. If an individual is brain

---

35   Hook and Mueller, "The Terri Schiavo Saga."

dead but has adequate renal, liver, pulmonary and cardiac function, then theoretically these organs, i.e., the kidneys, the liver, the lungs and the heart could be considered to be harvested for transplantation in order to save other patients' lives. Therefore, all human death is anatomically located in the brain.

Death is certified by a medical professional, at least in our cultures. In order to declare a person's death, there are various signs that signify death and are used by medical professionals to make the diagnosis. The International Classification of Diseases, Tenth Revision (ICD-10) lists 358 selected causes of death, which are used for tabulation and dissemination of mortality data by the National Center for Health Statistics (NCHS), recommended by the World Health Organization (WHO) for the purposes of identifying causes of death that are of public health and medical importance. To certify death, the medical practitioner has to rely on certain bodily criteria that signify death or shortly after death. It is not enough, however, to see a flatline on the monitor if a person is hospitalized or cessation of breathing by just looking at the body to verify death. The electrodes of the monitor might be disconnected, or the monitor might even show electrical signals in the absence of any cardiac function, for example if the patient has a pacemaker and the electrical impulses will still show up on the monitor despite the cessation of cardiac function. To verify death, it is usually required to document that there is no breathing activity over one minute or more (if the patient is not connected to a ventilator), there is no cardiac activity as measured by pulse or audible heart sounds for one minute or more, and if there is no response of the pupils to light (pupils are fixed) and no response to painful stimuli.

There are some signs of death, which are used by first responders to assess if someone can be or should be attempted to be saved by measures of cardiopulmonary resuscitation, besides absence of cardiac function, these are 1) decapitation, 2) decomposition of the entire body (not just of the extremities or parts of the skin), 3) rigor mortis or postmortem rigidity, which is a temporary stiffness that occurs hours after death before it vanishes after a few days, and 4) livor mortis or postmortem lividity, which is the accumulation of blood products in dependent portions under the skin appearing almost as bruises; (some authors add also as 5), burned beyond recognition).

In any of these scenarios, death is easily verifiable. Cardiac arrest is the classical sign of death. Brain death, on the other hand, is the irreversible damage of the brain tissue while other organs such as the heart might still be working. The diagnosis of brain death is important in transplant medicine and requires certain signs to verify before any organs could be retrieved for transplantation. A physician involved in a transplant surgery as the retriever of the organ or the surgeon performing the transplant of the donor organ into the recipient and any transplant physician cannot be legally involved in the diagnosis of brain death, at least in the US, Western Europe and most other (but not all) countries. The diagnosis of brain death requires the following three criteria to be present together: 1., persistent coma, 2., absence of brain stem reflexes, and 3., lack of ability to breath independently. To diagnose brain death has importance in order to certify irreversibility of brain damage, so that organs can be safely removed and used for transplantation purposes.

Among the general public, there always has been the fear that someone might be called brain dead while the person still might be able to recuperate and fully recover to a meaningful functional existence in life. In almost all cases, however, this vision is more the focus of science fiction and horror movies rather than reality in clinical practice. On the other hand, this fear is the reason for many to be reluctant to become organ donors. Moreover, the fear of premature burials let George Washington made his dead bed request not to be buried right away after his death but several days later in order to avoid hasty funeral arrangements.

In 2008, the US President's Council on Bioethics elaborated on a unifying medical concept of death. According to the Council, there is "a fundamental vital work of a living organism – the work of self-preservation, achieved through the organism's need-driven commerce with the surrounding world. For a human being, this commerce is manifested by the drive to breathe, demonstrating the most basic way a human being can act upon the world, combined with consciousness, or the ability to be open to the world. The irreversible loss of these two functions equates to human death".[36]

---

36   Gardiner et al., "International Perspective on the Diagnosis of Death."

Again, someone in a vegetative state, i.e., without consciousness but with maintained brain stem functions, is not brain dead, even though there might be no return of any consciousness expected, ever. Besides the standard physical examination that includes assessment of circulatory function, often routinely measured by auscultation of the heart using a stethoscope, evaluating the patients breathing activity using auscultation and visualization, sometime using a mirror or a feather in front of the mouth, and evaluation of brain function assessing eye reflexes to light or touch or painful stimuli, there are more sophisticated tests that can be done to ensure brain death. Such tests could be cerebral angiograms or transcranial Ultrasound Doppler to demonstrate the absence of blood flow to the brain, or electro encephalograms to demonstrate absence of any brain activity, or the apnea test. The apnea test has been considered a mandatory test to diagnoses brain death, a condition *sine qua non* for the determination of brain death, and it is usually performed on patients on a ventilator. One must consider that there are risks doing an apnea test and that the test is not reliable, and results can be misleading if the patient is on sedatives, narcotics or muscle relaxants or under the influence of drugs or alcohol or other toxins, which would influence the results.[37] If brain death is diagnosed, the person is considered dead, but then medications and ventilator therapy can be continued for the continued support of organ integrity for the purpose of transplantation alone. We will talk about organ transplantation again in a later chapter.

From a religious point of view, death is considered the relief of sin and sufferings ("those who died are set free of sin", Romans).

---

37   Machado, *Brain Death*.

Chapter Eleven

End of Life

D ying, on the other hand, is the relatively short lasting irreversible process that leads to death. Death marks the end of life, and the time and date of death is what is reported in the medical records. The end of life in its instance form in contrast to death, however, is a period between life and death, which is time-limited, whereas death is eternal. The date of death is of medical-legal importance for insurance purposes, pension payments, executions of legal wills, estate transfers, burial ceremonies among many other reasons. It marks the end of someone's life and the beginning of processes of grieving for family members or acquaintances, and the beginning of speaking of the past about someone who was but is no longer alive. Death is considered irreversible.

Almost every single person in the world encounters someone dying during their lifetime, usually a family member, especially someone's grandparents first because of their advanced age, followed by the death of someone's parents. Therefore, the experience of death is part of our common life, our culture, and our existence. According to many, the hardest thing about death is actually not the death itself, but the fact that there is no going back, and there is no more direct communication with the person who passed away, not in person, not over the phone, not in writing to each other, not on a Zoom call. Death is the end of communication, at least the type of communication we are used to among human beings. Therefore, death is also the end of personal getting togethers; a person alive cannot any longer enjoy the direct company of someone who had died and cannot share meals and drinks and gifts and events. The dead person only stays in the memories of the remaining living people. Death is the end of life for the person who died, but also for the environment of that person including his or her home, family, friends, colleagues, hobbies or work. Everything that was affected by the person who died during his or her lifetime stopped with the death. The end of life in this context means also the end of work, of all activities, of all creativity, of all physicalities, and of all mental, emotional and spiritual interactions, except those that might be existent - or not existent - after death.

One of the main determinants for the difference between life and death besides the above is – time. Time is changing - all the time. Time is never steady. Nothing is permanent, except change (as wisely stated by Heraclitus of Ephesus, around 500 B.C.), and time. Time is somewhat permanent since it is always there - but never ever the same and therefore, always changing, all the time.

Life is a function of time. Without time, there would be no growth, no development, no degeneration, no death. The end of life is also a function of time, and thus, limited as time is. Time is limited but also permanent, life is limited and could also be permanent, if recurrent in other organisms, but not in the same.

Our earthly existence is limited, and everything what we encounter during our lifetime, is limited, and goes away. One could argue therefore, that death and the end of life could be limited, too, but this has never been demonstrated in a scientific context, so far, for the individual. But for the whole of nature, creation, and universal energy, even death is not timeless, but a process that is leading to another process.

Chapter Twelve

Near Death Experiences

There have been uncountable reports and descriptions of experiences people had at a time when they were at the bridge to death, - but survived. Of interest, the vast majority of these accounts sound relatively similar in type and nature, which make many believe that these individuals had a glimpse of death and the beyond. Many sound more like a dream rather than a nightmare. Interdisciplinary scientific analysis was attempted by many to explore these experiences in order to figure out if someone could really see what is coming after earthly life. One common feature for all is the phenomenon of the bright light. The second feature is that according to those who experienced near death experiences, nobody mentioned that it was scary and frightening, just the opposite. The question is, however, what does this really mean? Is what people see a glimpse of death or the afterlife? Or is this just an imaginary trick our brain plays caused by lack of oxygen and accumulation of toxic metabolites that may cause hallucinations as part of a cell-protective mechanisms to shut down consciousness in view of tissue damage?

Near death experiences have been described in details in many publications, according to Bailey and Yates (The Near Death Experience, 1996), there are different types mentioned and categorized, even though these appear smore as different experiences such as hearing voices, reviewing one's owns life experiences, seeing or meeting others close to oneself, seeing dark tunnels followed by bright lights, among others[38]. According to an analysis by George Gallup in 1982, approximately 15% of Americans (23 million people) had some kind of death encounters with 8 million having some sort of mystical experience[39]. Of interest is that in many cases people who had those experiences saw this as a call for a significant life change, such as the story of a drug addict who almost died and then became sober and devoted her life as a drug counselor, they were somewhat "transformed by the light" (Melvin Morse, 1992)[40]. Near death experiences are oftentimes referred to as transcendent experiences or heaven-like experiences while only a small proportion (<1%) reported distressing hell-like or torment visions.

Whether near death experiences do really represent a glimpse into the next world or whether these phenomena are just a result of lack of oxygen in the brain or accumulated endorphins representing metabolic induced hallucinations (such as certain drugs like opiates might do) or whether a mental disorganization as a cerebral defense mechanisms creates vivid thoughts, detachment, memories and visions remains controversially discussed, but its conformity in presence and lack of data showing similar findings in experimental lack of oxygen or opioid use makes it more intriguing to believe that it might represent a vision of dying - rather than of death or rather than of the afterlife.

---

38   Bailey and Yates, *The Near-Death Experience*.
39   *Adventures in Immortality by George Gallup*.
40   "Transformed By the Light."

Chapter Thirteen

Eschatology

E schatology is the science within theology of the very last things, whether it relates to the world, to humanity, or to the individual (individual eschatology). While theology deals with faith seeking reason (or understanding, = *fides quaerens intellectum*), eschatology is the doctrine of the final destiny of where God's creation ends up. Eschatology does not – in contrast to some beliefs – deal with something after death but is evident in our here and now. *Escaton* is the end of the world.

Eschatology is the main doctrine defining Christology since Jesus Christ promises the Kingdom to come. The early Christians, therefore, were awaiting the second coming of the Messiah, the Kingdom in Christ to come soon after Jesus' death and resurrection. Christian hope is concerned with the science of the last things. Eschatology in this sense deals with the end of the world, the climax of all negativities, redemption, leading then to the prophesied future of re-birth or the promised union with the divine, right after the days of final judgement.

Outside religious borders, eschatology in general deals also with human extinction and the end of life on planet earth, caused by global catastrophes such as a nuclear war or meteorite collision or infectious disease outbreaks (sound too familiar in our times, doesn't it?). The Oxford English Dictionary defines eschatology as "part of theology concerned with death, judgment, and the final destiny of the soul and humankind".

If we discuss death, mortality, and immortality, we are basically dealing purely with what eschatology deals with, in particular individual eschatology, meaning the end of the individual person's life. The eschatological approach to the end of life and time, is manifold, and mainly philosophical in its natural roots, but more religious in living practice, since so far, only religious faith can provide the hope for whatever is to come after the end – "*the hope for the future*" as Joseph Cardinal Ratzinger (Pope Benedict XVI) called it in his highly recognized textbook on Eschatology - at least until biology might prevail.

The eschatological idea is a restoration of all things, according to Peter in Acts. The defeat of death, the undoing of death is the ultimate goal, which is achieved by the *Parousia*, the coming or arrival of Christ on earth, or what many call the 2nd coming.

The main concept of Christian eschatology, as interpreted form St Paul's letters in the New Testament such as Corinthians 15, is not for us human beings going to heaven when we die, but that Christ is coming down from heaven to earth – in contrast to common beliefs, "the heavenly city descending from heaven to earth". The corruptible mortal body is clothed in incorruption and immortality, then "death is swallowed up in victory" (Phillip Cary, History of Christian Theology, The Great Courses), and the body then becomes a spiritual, heavenly body that is everlasting.[41]

The eschatological future in Christian faith is purely based on the resurrection of Christ, so our (human) hope is the resurrection of every one of us (or maybe not for everyone) - after we die. In that sense, the eschatological expectation is to exist forever in a heavenly home *in spe*, and heaven therefore is where eternal life is already, but not yet for us. The question always remains, who will go to heaven and who will not. Christians believe that a just and moral life in Jesus Christ will prepare us to an eternal life. Religious living in its totality such as those in monasticism, have the objective to imitate the life of Jesus Christ as far as possible in preparation for attaining eternal life after death.

---

41   *The History of Christian Theology.*

In April 2021, Cyril O'Regan published a well-received commentary on Ratzinger's eschatology, which has become the standard textbook for Catholic theology over the last decades: *"...he* (Ratzinger) *articulates his vision of Christian hope against the backdrop of the gravity of our being torn from this earth, at once beautiful and cruel, the scene of our greatest betrayals as well as loves, and undergoing a frightful disintegration that reason takes to be final."*[42]

The later Pope Benedict XVI hereby declares that eschatology defines everyone's end of life and death, in one way or another. The end of life and the end of the existence of the earthly world is linked to the person Jesus Christ, the son of God, part of the divine trinity, and with this Christology, the end might be coupled to the second coming of Christ and the coming of the Kingdom of God on earth. With this thoughts, the Kingdom is lifted off the shoulders of mankind since it is directed by Christ as per the New Testament.

"The power of death means that the transcendent dimension remains enduringly relevant. In Eschatology Ratzinger wished to maintain a distinction between the kingdom of God and the kingdom of the world....Ratzinger judges that an interpretive stance overdetermined by political rectification yields to the temptation of confusing the kingdom of God with the kingdom of the world".

...No person can call herself Christian if she fails to recognize the dignity of all and fails to wish eternal life for all.... Death is also the site of the irreversible judgment as to whether one lived in truth or in the lie."

Of interest, at one point, life becomes the practice of death, either in case of incurable deadly diseases such as advanced stages of cancer or in progressive frailty at old age, where life might purely deal with the basics of biology such as nutrition and digestion and then turn towards silence, memories, and waiting for the end - and beyond. For people of faith, this period might be filled with prayers or meditation (on the divine, Hans Urs von Balthazar), while for those without faith - if not for all - the unimaginable end might be troubled with anxiety, fear, search for answers and a blind trust for those close or caregivers in hospital and nursing home or hospice settings.

Even here nature has provided man with biologic protection in the way our mind shuts down, unconsciousness or confusion might over-

---

42   O'Regan, "Benedict XVI."

come to take us away from the brutal reality of our demise, even shock and multi-organ failure might occur that alleviates pain and sufferings by shutting down consciousness using toxic metabolites and cellular acidosis as a result of lack of oxygen resulting in a deep sleep that then opens the gate to death – and eternity.

Of importance, eschatology in its purest theological form – at least in Christianity, is concerned with the last things, death, judgement, heaven, and hell. It can be evaluated mainly academic as Ratzinger does, as a warning for a moral life (as per conditional immortality) or as a bridge to hope for an eternal life as Kueng sees it. This hope is essential to Catholic Theology, it is the way to deal with the incomprehensibility of God and whatever might come to us after our life ends, for the coming of a new heaven and new earth (Revelation 21:1), which includes the promise of the personal salvation of each of us, the physical resurrection of our materiality - rather than only our spirituality, and the saving of our community as an entity - rather than loneliness in heaven.[43]

Moreover, modernity has brought forward a form of secular eschatology that evaluates the history of humanity with the absence of any theological aspects as in Marxism, as an example. In our current time, the overwhelming and occasionally exaggerated trust in scientific schemes by our modern society leaves hardly any room for God or religion, until the individual self is affected at a time when no more science can comfort the transition from the live here to whatever is succeeding and wherever that might be, if anything. Eschaton, the final destination for either the cosmic or for the individual end, might be the defeat of death, which would be the absolute meaning of immortality. The eschaton is not the continuation of our earthly existence, it will not be a condition that was the same as it was but now miraculously is just better, and it is not becoming harp playing cherubs sitting on white clouds. The real eschaton might be within us, as it might be the same for the kingdom of God.

---

43   Bauerschmidt and Buckley, *Catholic Theology.*

Chapter Fourteen

Immortality and Bioethics

Bioethics is a relatively new faculty that emerged as a result of moral-ethical concerns using animals for medical and biologic experiment sin the 1970s. From there, bioethics became a science and practice to protect human beings in medicine and research based on the following pillars of thought: 1. Patient Autonomy, 2. Beneficence, 3. nonmaleficense, and 4. social justice. These principles form the work that is supposed to ensure protection of the human being, his integrity and health and dignity within the necessities undergoing medical care and treatments.

In clinical practice the two main scenarios where I personally face bioethical issues are 1) cases of futile care, and 2) research protocols.

Futility or futile care in medicine is defined as the utilization of medical resources that are not going to change the patient's condition or the outcome, mostly in end-of-life situations. An extreme example would be to perform open heart surgery in a 90 year-old patient who had a cardiac arrest and is suffering from irreversible brain damage and irreversible multiorgan failure in a coma. In such a case, surgery might be technically feasible in experienced hands of a skillful surgeon and might work, however, the patient likely will not wake up from the coma, his brain will not miraculously heal and his irreversible multiorgan failure is not improving, just the opposite, a patient like that is likely going to die within hours to a few days. I am mentioning this particular example since it does represent a real case that I personally have encountered a few years ago, in which the patient's family, though relatively well-educated, did not want to accept the medical facts and requested that everything being done to save the patient's life. No heart surgeon I know would have taken such a patient to the operating room for a futile surgical open-heart operation which likely could have killed the patient even hours earlier as a result of the procedure. The family, however, insisted and threatened to sue all doctors on his case if we would not perform the surgery. A threat like this is not as rare as the public might think, but thank God, nobody can force a physician to perform a surgery if he or she does not think that this would be in the patient's best interest. In this case, I called for an urgent bioethics consult. Every hospital should have a bioethics team or dedicated physicians who then can evaluate the case from a medical point of view and form a bioethical point of view and then give their recommendations, but also initiate a meeting with the family and talk to them with or without all doctors involved in the case. If requested by the patient beforehand or the family, a clerical individual such as a priest or rabbi might be involved in such a discussion. In this particular case, the patient's family did not agree with any of our recommendations and then in turn requested a transfer of the patient to another medical facility. Even though most of the doctors working on the patient's case, also were attending physicians at the other academic medical center the family requested, there was absolute no way to have that patient transferred, for the following reasons:

1. The patient s was clinically way too unstable to get him into an ambulance and drive him across town to get to another hospital.
2. Therefore, I as the attending physician on this case, did not agree and did not order the transfer.
3. Even if some else would have tried, no ambulance drivers would have agreed to take such an unstable, dying patient into their ambulance, since nobody wants to have to report a death during transportation.

4. The receiving hospital would not have accepted the patient, anyhow, since usually there are no intensive care (or any other telemetry) beds available right away, but most higher level of care facilities have long waiting lists from other hospital for transfers, and only patients who might likely benefit from the higher level of care, have priority.

5. The patient's insurance company had no contract with the requested hospital, therefore the patient's insurance did not agree with the transfer, and the receiving hospital did not agree with the acceptance of the patient.

6. The requested hospital would not have accepted the patient independent on all of the above just because of his current condition since any reasonable physician would understand the end-of-life situation.

Despite our repeated conversations with the patient's family, they started cursing and became very accusatory, which is also not an uncommon finding when people try to find someone to blame for a grave medical condition. They left the room during the last meeting shouting and yelling at everyone and threatening all of us, and also stated that they know doctors at the other hospital, and they will take the patient out themselves against medical advice and drive hm to the other facility. I assume that they then talked to someone at the other hospital, since a few hours later I received a call form one of my colleagues from that hospital to inquire about the patient and his condition. The doctor was an intensivist who I knew very well since many years, and he instantaneously understood the situation and agree with us, and he informed the family thereafter, that he would not be able to accept the patient. Within a few hours, the patient expired as excepted. Instead of spending the last hours of his life at his bedside to provide support to the comatose individual, the family attempted to aggressively challenge what a common mind easily could have understood or what a team of highly educated and well-trained medical professionals provided to their best of knowledge and experience. At least, the patient did not know anything about this, he even had a written will singed by him beforehand that he did not want to undergo any major surgeries or procedures if they are considered futile. For all health care providers involved in this particular case, this was a horrifying experience, and for medical legal reasons, we were glad to have had bioethics involved and to have their written documentation in the patient's electronic medical records.

This was a not so rare case in which a patient's relatives requested care considered futile in a dying patient - against all recommendations from health care providers. Common sense and a bit of understanding of biology and medicine should be sufficient to understand when a 90 year old might be at the end of his life, but obviously sometimes some people might believe that doctors could provide immortality - even if it is by performing risky surgeries. Please be aware that the age itself is absolutely not a contraindication against any surgery, not even heart surgery, since we have performed several procedures in people even above 100 years of age. But in many cases at the end of life, a risky surgery in fact might have had elucidated some long-term benefit if conducted 10 years earlier while the patient was in a relatively healthy stable condition, but not in a situation such as the current one in our above example.

One should keep in mind that there are only two reasons to perform any risky surgeries (such as open-heart surgery) at any age and in any patient: 1. To alleviate symptoms if patients suffer, and 2. To prolong life if the condition otherwise represents a constant danger to life (what we might call a "time bomb" when we talk to patients, such as a very severe symptomatic aortic valve stenosis, as an example). In most cases in the very elderly, however, prolongation of life is likely not a reasonable justification since they might have already surpassed their average age life expectancy but improvement of symptoms is (such as chest pain or shortness of breath or intractable arrhythmia among a few others).

There are many other situations in which health care providers need bioethics involved in the care of patients. Recently more often than ever before, I have encountered patient cases in which treatment decisions needed to be made in individuals who were unable to decide on their own (since they might have been comatose or sedated, or mentally unable to do so). If there are no relatives or a power of attorney, then physicians have to make their own decisions based on their understanding what the patient might have wanted, which is oftentimes impossible to guess. I had a case like that recently where a male patient in his mid seventies had a survived cardiac arrest, was at the time I was involved in the care, sedated, intubated, on a ventilator and had no family and also had never appointed a power of attorney to make medical decisions on his behalf. He had a complete heart block with a resulting heart rate of approximately 30 beats per minute, which itself represents an absolute indication for a mechanical pacemaker implantation. For a pacemaker implantation, however, the proceduralist needs a signed informed consent, since the surgery even though considered low risk, in rare cases can have serious complications (in less than 1%). As in many cases, one has to make a decision Saturday night when not everyone who is involved in the patient's care is reachable so that there might be a lack of information. The physician then might just go ahead with the surgery of a pacemaker implantation since it could save the patient's life. This would be the scenario, most likely, anywhere in Europe. In the US, however, in view of the huge plentitude of lawsuits against physicians, most doctors would hold off, until either a judge has appointed a power of attorney for the case (which is not done Saturday night), or a bioethics consult has been obtained, which then might support the physicians, decisions for or against a procedure without consent, but with *"implied consent"*. Again, the reason to get bioethics involved is primarily for ethical-moral reasons to provide the best possible care without affecting a patient's autonomy in medical decision making and also for medical legal reasons in cases as this one. In this particular case, I did ask for a bioethics consult which I then received Sunday morning and an hour later, I took the patient to the operation theater to implant a pacemaker. I guess the patient and the medical team also were lucky that the patient survived the night. The patient actually did extremely well after the procedure, was weaned off the ventilator the following day and was able to leave the hospital to a skilled nursing facility a few days thereafter. In this case, the patient initially was not in a condition to ask for it, but a surgical procedure did in fact, prolong his life.

Prolongation of life is not the same as immortality. Immortality, in a biologic sense, cannot be expected at the actual end-of life of a human being, despite advances in anti-aging and immortality research popularized from basic scientific laboratories or the write up from technology-driven futurists. In other words, to work on biologic immortality does not begin at the end of life in an intensive care unit when organs are failing and irreversible damage has occurred already, but years before degenerative processes of aging are at a point of no return. Nobody knows, however, when that would be, probably this might be very early in life, latest in mid adulthood, I suppose.

Chapter Fifteen

Philosophical Considerations on Immortality

I mmortality is defined as the indefinite continuation of existence, even beyond one's life on earth.[44,45] Oftentimes, immortality is called *everlasting life*, which somehow is related to time (eternity), whereas *eternal life* is more time-independent. *Biological immortality* refers to the possibility of a bodily life extension regarding advances in anti-aging research. Immortality for a human being, however, always should be considered for both body and soul. Whereas a bodily or biological immortality seems still be far away from anything a human could achieve at the current time, both philosophy and religion focus on the possibility of a continuous existence of the soul or possibly the soul and the body after the bodily death.

The concept of an immortal soul dates to Plato who saw the body as a transient matter deemed to be degenerating in time while the soul is the spirit that might live on forever in a space beyond our current understanding, even after the bodily demise. Even before Plato, Alcmaeon of Croton

---

44   Ritchie, "Theories of Immortality."
45   Borges and Weinberger, "Immortality."

argued that the soul is a never-ending energy. In Plato's Phaedo, four theories for the immortality of the soul are described: the *Cyclical Argument*, the *Theory of Recollection*, the *Affinity Argument*, and the *Argument from Form of Life*.[46] The basic idea is that the soul is simple and therefore, cannot be destroyed and must be immortal.

The idea of immortality, according to the Russian novelist Fyodor Dostojevsky (1821-1881), is the *"fundamental and highest idea of human existence"*.[47] From a Platonic point of view, immortality of the soul is key to understand the ongoing existence of our earthly existence in a different space.

Rene Descartes (1596-1650), the French philosopher and mathematician who invented analytic geometry, believed that the human being is composed of two substances, the material body substance and the mental substance (the soul), which is the basis for the *"Cartesian dualism"*.[48] The mental substance represents the thoughts, which are immaterial and leave the body after death. However, the Cartesian dualism has been heavily criticized and is rejected by many philosophers today.

Modern philosophy created the movement of *transhumanism*, which anticipates that the human race will join together with artificial intelligence, transcending the human being into another (computerized) sphere (the H+ Community).[49] By use of machines and computers the ultimate goal is the preserve and advance mental capacity and intelligence.

The development of artificial intelligence (AI) technologies is supposed to improve human sensory reception, emotive ability, and cognitive capacity. As such, a combined AI/human being would then have prolonged health and longevity, if not immortality, possibly leading to what is called technological *singularity*, [50,51,52] which is an explosion of intellectual capacity surpassing all human intelligence. According to the well-known physicist Stephen Hawk-

---

46   Palmer, *The Method of Hypothesis and the Nature of Soul in Plato's Phaedo*.
47   Scanlan, "Dostoevsky's Arguments for Immortality."
48   Cottingham, *The Cambridge Companion to Descartes*.
49   Fukuyama, "Transhumanism."
50   Fukuyama.
51   CORDEIRO, "From Biological To Technological Evolution."
52   Frey, "DEMYSTIFYING THE FUTURE."

ing (1942-2018), full artificial intelligence could result in human extinction in the not far future.[53]

Human Enhancement

In order to gain prolongation of life or even immortality, there is a need for a change in the natural process of aging and degeneration. Human enhancement in this sense means to develop and improve the human being at its current stage by different means using life-style, technologies, medicine and scientific advances.[54]

There are different forms of human enhancement: reproductive enhancements include embryo selection in order to avoid genetic diseases or better, to early diagnose existence of certain conditions. Physical enhancements include several changes whether it is by using cosmetics or dietary supplements (to look better or to loose excessive weight), functional improvements including the use of performance enhancing agents (to achieve more physical and functional gain in sports, as an example), the use of prosthetics (artificial limbs after accidental loss), medical devices such as pacemakers or defibrillators to overcome (age-related) degeneration of our heart's electrical system or even to prevent sudden death.

In addition, external devices such as laptops or smart phones are used to enhance cognitive and social abilities that are in heavy consumption, while personal drones and on-body and in-body nanonetworks or 3-D bioprinting for further human technological enhancements are already developed and currently fine-tuned to be ready for large scale utilization within the coming years.[55]

Transhumanism

To look way beyond our human existence in its current version, *transhumanism* represents a theory that evolved into a philosophical movement which tries to eliminate all human limitations and increases longevity as well as cog-

53   "Stephen Hawking: Stephen Hawking Warned Artificial Intelligence Could End Human Race - The Economic Times."
54   Pound and Miah, "Human Enhancement."
55   Dickel and Schrape, "Dezentralisierung, Demokratisierung, Emanzipation."

nitive and intellectual enhancement. Its core is the development of the evolution of an intelligent species beyond the human capabilities known to date.[56]

Transhumanism is distinctive in its particular focus on the applications of technologies to the improvement of human bodies at the individual level. Many transhumanists actively assess the potential for future technologies and innovative social systems to improve the quality of all life, while seeking to make the material reality of the human condition fulfill the promise of legal and political equality by eliminating congenital mental and physical barriers.

Transhumanist philosophers argue that there not only exists a so-called "perfectionist ethical imperative" for humans to strive for progress and improvement of the human condition, but that it is possible and desirable for humanity to enter into a phase of existence in which humans develop beyond what is naturally considered human. In such a phase, natural evolution would be replaced with deliberate participatory or directed evolution.

Posthumanism

Posthumanism, on the other hand, is an ideology and movement which seeks to develop and make available technologies that completely eliminate processes and consequences of aging, enable immortality and greatly enhance human intellectual, physical and psychological capabilities, in order to develop a post-human, human-artificial species.[57]

Both the concepts of Transhumanism and Posthumanism one might consider as *techno-quantum mechanical* in nature and thus, have no obvious place for religion, spirituality or personal faith.

There are other ideas of whatever might come after our well known but so limited life on earth. Some speculate a life without human interaction, since humans will be extinct at one time anyhow, but certain animals might life free in a natural environment, that humans can no longer destroy further, so that *nature can take its course* (without humans), as postulated by the

---

56   Fukuyama, "Transhumanism."
57   Remshardt, "Posthumanism."

paleontologist Dougal Dixon in his description *After Man: A Zoology of the Future,* in 1998.[58]

In his speculative fiction entitled *Theory for the World to Come,* Matthew Wolf-Meyer elaborates on this idea and further talks about the *"madness gene"* that makes humans to search for a new world, a new technology, a new cosmos, a new universe, for immortality. That what he and others called the madness gene is nothing else than our own spirit, our drive, our energy that is not meant to be just a mindless existence, but the drive for modern technology and discovery, the ambition to reach the unreachable, to fly to Moon and Mars, but this also can lead to individual failure, to death, and lastly possibly even to the end not only of the individual but also for the entire human race. [59]

Is living in harmony with nature healthier than searching over and over again for the unknown, the innovation, the unthinkable? It might be healthier for the earth and the present, but the search for the unexplainable must go on to find new technologies.

58   Dixon, *After Man.*
59   Wolf-Meyer, *Theory for the World to Come.*

Chapter Sixteen

Religious Considerations on Immortality

Christianity

Immortality in a philosophical and religious sense means the indefinite continuation of existence, especially of the soul after death. Immortality in philosophy is also called the *afterlife*, but this terminology would distinguish life before and after death rather than a continuation of earthly existence.

In Christianity, however, the death and resurrection of Jesus Christ does not represent immortality in its purest sense. Christ - according to the Scriptures in the New Testament - did die on the cross, and it was not his soul that survived. In contrast, his body had risen from the dead to live again as a human but divine being, with a body and soul. The immortality of Jesus Christ is the resurrection from the dead in the same body rather than a continuation of his live despite his murder. Christianity teaches the Kingdom of God in heaven coming to earth with those believing being resurrected to eternal life. It is not the eternity of the soul but the eternity of the human body and the soul as one entity.

In a way, however, Christian religion proposes the bodily immortality rather than the survival of the soul, even though this thought has been forgotten by many believers and worshippers, obviously mainly because of the unbelievable and incomprehensible idea of immortality of the person as a whole.

There are three distinct differences even in a philosophical view of bodily immortality: the survival of an astral body resembling the physical body; the immortality of the immaterial soul (that is an incorporeal existence); and the resurrection of the body (or re-embodiment, in case the resurrected person does not keep the same body as at the moment of death).

Again, the Biblical Scriptures do not teach any of those ideas but speak of the same body of the same person with the same mind and soul achieving eternal life.

Christianity therefore teaches the existence of immortality after death, which then became the goal of alchemy to search for scientific clues to induce immortality by defying the occurrence of death. Alchemy initially intended to create gold from cheap metals, which has never succeeded. Alchemy also intended to find the fountain of youth, or a miracle elixir for an ever-lasting life. [60]

Eschatology is the part of (Christian) theology that deals with the end, the end of the world, or the final events in history such as the end of humanity, but also with the end of life, and death. Individual eschatology represents the Christian theological doctrine of man's end of life and life after death of the soul (rather than an afterlife of the bodily individual).

Christianity gives importance to life after death as a promise to be achieved for those who know how to keep the doctrinal precepts that are thought. A notorious distinction between the Old and the New Testament is the concept of immortality of the body (mentioned to be destined to transform into light before going to heaven), and the immortality of the soul (which is not even mentioned on the Old Testament). Death is broadly mentioned in the Bible, emphasizing the fragility of the physical body *("flesh")* and the incorruptibility and the perpetuity of the spirit, implying immortality in the physical body as an unattainable possibility *(Genesis 3:19)*, also as a unique attribute of God that cannot be given to men on this life *(1 Timothy 6:16)* but will be granted in the afterlife.

---

60   Straus, "Alchemy."

Christian teachings refer to death as a triumph, and encourages the pursuit of it because there is no happiness in this life greater than that to be obtained by dwelling in heaven after death *(1 Corinthians 15:53-54, 2 Corinthians 5:1-2)*, this tied to a conditional immortality, that can only be achieved with strict adherence to Christian beliefs and commandments, meaning only those who persevere in good deeds and avoid sin *(Romans 2:6-7)*.

- Genesis 3:19
  In the sweat of thy face shalt thou eat bread, till thou return unto the ground; for out of it wast thou taken: for dust thou art, and unto dust shalt thou return.
- 1 Timothy 6:16
  Who only hath immortality, dwelling in the light which no man can approach unto; whom no man hath seen, nor can see: to whom *be* honour and power everlasting. Amen.
- 1 Corinthians 15:53-54
  For this corruptible must put on incorruption, and this mortal must put on immortality. So, when this corruptible shall have put on incorruption, and this mortal shall have put on immortality, then shall be brought to pass the saying that is written, Death is swallowed up in victory.
- 2 Corinthians 5:1-2
  For we know that if our earthly house of this tabernacle were dissolved, we have a building of God, a house not made with hands, eternal in the heavens. For in this we groan, earnestly desiring to be clothed upon with our house which is from heaven.
- Romans 2:6-8
  Who will render to every man according to his deeds: To them who by patient continuance in well doing seek for glory, honour and immortality, eternal life: But unto them that are contentious, and do not obey the truth, but obey the unrighteousness, indignation and wraith.

According to the fathers of the Catholic Church like Augustine of Hippo (354-430) and Thomas Aquinas (1225-1274), the soul or spirit gives the breath of life to the body. According to Catholic tradition, the soul itself cannot exist without the body, therefore the soul has to reunite with the body or transfer on to a different bodily form.

The immortality on the soul has not been described in the Scriptures, instead, according to Christian belief, is described as resurrection from the dead, as evidence with Jesus's resurrection after his death.

The idea of dualism in general makes it easy for believers to have faith in an immortal soul, i.e., the existence of the immortal non-substantial mind or spirit in a space beyond our imagination. The immortality of the soul, however, as mentioned above, is not mentioned in the Scriptures, at all.

Soul in a Christian sense, is associated with the energy that gives life, or the breath that makes the body a living substance.

According to Thomas Aquinas, the greatest Doctor of the Catholic Church and main representative of scholasticism, the soul is the principle of life, therefore every living thing has a soul. The human soul is called a rational soul which has intelligence and consciousness and reason, which is somehow synonymous with spirit. Aquinas also states that the human being is vitalized and energized by its soul which makes the body a functional substance (rather than a lifeless corpse)[61].

The soul in this context is the biological driver and organizer of the living being. The rational soul therefore is closely connected to the body, meaning the body cannot live without the soul. All our activities are function of our organs, except the two spiritual activities knowing and loving, which are rendered by intellect and will, which is a spiritual power, belonging to the soul. But the soul on the other hand, can live outside the body since the soul has this spiritual power, in addition to its role in energizing and organizing the body. Therefore, according to Aquinas, the soul can live outside the body, and can exist after the body dies.

Therefore, the soul is immortal, from a Catholic point of view.

---

61   Aquinas, *The Summa Theologica of St. Thomas Aquinas.*

Islam

The fundamental notion of Islam (similar to Christianity) is that the beginning of humanity is a divine creation and narrates that the temptation of man is a focal theme[62]. Those who surrender to Allah have a way to avoid this temptation. The concept of immortality starts with Allah, the Cherisher and sustainer of the world. This is believed from the inference derived from the Quran where Allah says in Surat *Al-Mujadilah 58:11* "Allah will exalt those who believe among you, and those who have knowledge, to high ranks."

- Ar-Rum 30:11
- Allah originates the creation, then He will repeat it, then to Him you will be returned.
- Sahih Bukhari book Vol. 8, Book 73, Hadith 155 Prophet Mohammed says "your body has a right on you".

With the progression of Islam in the 7th century, sparks of scientific knowledge evolved the way medicine was perceived. Ibn Al Nafis, a Muslim physician, expressed pulmonary circulation 300 years before William Harvey[63]. Abu Al Qassim AlZahrawi's text became the leading medical resource for European universities. Al Razi and Ibn Sina were known as pioneers in the field of medicine. The holistic approach we now use in modern medicine was initially described by these Muslim physicians. Islam has always represented to be an advocate for developments in science and the art of the human body.

In Surat Fatir verse 28, Allah describes that the most fearful of Allah are the most knowledgeable in advances of science. (Only those of His slaves' fear Allah who are knowledgeable - 35:28).

With the emergence of Islam, there was always a great emphasis placed on development in the scientific discipline. The immense importance placed on knowledge, cure of disease, alongside the pursuit of scientific develop-

62   Ghayas and Batool, "Construction and Validation of Afterlife Belief Scale for Muslims."
63   Masic, "On Occasion of 800th Anniversary of Birth of Ibn Al-Nafis--Discoverer of Cardiac and Pulmonary Circulation."

ment, there is not much conflicted exhibited in increasing one's longevity as the Prophet (ﷺ) says (*Allah has not sent any disease without sending a cure for it*). This is also supported by the Prophet (ﷺ) Narrated by Abu al-Darda: The Prophet (ﷺ) said: Allah has sent down both the disease and the cure, and He has appointed a cure for every disease, so treat yourselves medically, but use nothing unlawful[64].

On the other hand, in the literal terms of immortality, the Noble Quran clearly states that every human being shall taste death in one manner or another. (3:185) Every human being is bound to taste death: and you shall receive your rewards in full on the Day of Resurrection. He who is kept away from the Fire and is admitted to Paradise, will surely triumph; for the life of this world is nothing but an illusory enjoyment.

Finally, Allah clearly indicates in Surat Yunis that we have the power to heal (*O mankind! There has come to you a good advice from your Lord (i.e., the Qur'an), and a healing for that which is in your hearts.*)

Hinduism

In Hinduism, the concept of immortality revolves around the mind and the soul. The immortal soul is explained through births and rebirths, as it traverses through various physical bodies to progress its endless journey[65].

Almost all belief systems around the globe think time is linear. Hinduism perceives time as a cycle and not as a linear progression. A macrocycle (yuga) lasts for four million plus years, and a microcycle (samvatsara) is restricted to a person's lifetime[66]. The Yuga Cycle (time cycle) is in four phases, starting from Krita Yuga, Treta Yuga, Dvapara Yuga, and Kali Yuga[67]. The belief is that every living being will be born with a different name and form and progresses his cosmic accounting book.

64   Khan, *The Translation of the Meanings of Summarized Sahih Al-Bukhari*.
65   ThriftBooks, "A Brief Introduction to Hinduism."
66   Mukundananda, "Chapter 2, Verse 20 – Bhagavad Gita, The Song of God – Swami Mukundananda."nor
       does it ever die; nor having once existed, does it ever cease to be. The … Commentary: The eternal nature of
       the soul has been established in this verse, which is ever-existing and beyond birth and death. Consequently,
       it is devoid of …","language":"en","title":"Chapter 2, Verse 20 – Bhagavad Gita, The Song of God – Swami
       Mukundananda","URL":"https://www.holy-bhagavad-gita.org/chapter/2/verse/20","author":[{"family":"Mukundananda
       ","given":"Swami"}],"accessed":{"date-parts":[["2021",11,23]]}}}],"schema":"https://github.com/citation-style-language/
       schema/raw/master/csl-citation.json"}
67   V, "The Four Yugas and Their Significance."

The cosmic accounting book essentially has two entries: 1. with the depositing credit they are born with, and 2. what they accumulate or lose in the current lifetime.

We often hear stories about people being extraordinarily talented in a particular field starting from early childhood itself. This brilliance can be explained by this method of accounting. In essence, the souls are the same; it is the physical being that is changed. The reason for cremation also, in a way, supports this concept. The Hindu religion is depicted in numerous works of literature and scripts and is considered a vast territory.

This study is focusing on few significant viewpoints that are discussed below.

Bhagavad Gita: Many verses describe the Soul as being immortal in the Gita. One such verse -

> na jāyate mriyate vā kadāchin
>> nāyaṁ bhūtvā bhavitā vā na bhūyaḥ
>> ajo nityaḥ śāśhvato 'yaṁ purāṇo
>> na hanyate hanyamāne śharīre

This verse translates to: The soul is neither born nor does it ever die, nor having once existed, does it ever cease to be. The soul is without birth, eternal, immortal, and ageless. It is not destroyed when the body is destroyed.

Amritam is considered an antidote to death - It is said that whoever drinks it becomes immortal. It is described as an elixir drunk by gods that granted them immortality.

Katha Upanishad

In Katha Upanishad, the famous conversation between Nachiketa (a teen boy) and the god of death Yama is described below: The all-knowing Self was never born, nor will it die. Beyond cause and effect, this Self is eternal. When the body dies, the Self does not die.

Brihadaranyaka Upanishad (the nature of reality and the identity of the Self, or Atman)

'When a lump of salt is thrown into the water, it dissolves and cannot be removed even though we can taste the salty water.' So, the separate Soul dissolves in the sea of pure consciousness, infinite and immortal. Separateness comes when we identify the Self with the body; when this physical identification dissolves, the Self is no longer separate.

Chiranjeevee

Chiranjeevee means a long-living person. There are eight such people. The samvatsara of life and death is endless until one finds liberation, or Moksha states the Hindu way of life. Until the elusive Moksha is attained either by good karma or nirvana, life goes on between birth and death.

Hamsa Upanishad and longevity

In the search for immortality, many sages and hermits practice different forms of yogic life, including Hatha Yoga and Kundalini Yoga. The central idea behind this is to control the breathing rate. Hamsa translates to "That I am," meaning I am the same as the universe [24]. The Hamsa Upanishad says that an average human performs 21,460 breaths (15 breaths/minute x 60 minutes/hour x 24 hours/day). There was a quest to decrease the breathing rate by observing the breaths to attain immortality. After adapting to yoga and meditation, improvements in biomarkers of cellular aging and longevity were demonstrated in one recent research[68]. On researching more about this domain, few individuals living over 100 years of age. One such person is Swami Sivananda from Varanasi – A spirited monk putting his longevity down to a disciplined Yoga life[69]. The practice of slow breathing appears to optimize many physiological parameters of the respiratory, cardiovascular, and autonomic nervous systems, leading to longevity[70]. These practices could a starting point to prove yoga and meditation may actually delay aging.

---

68   Tolahunase, Sagar, and Dada, "Impact of Yoga and Meditation on Cellular Aging in Apparently Healthy Individuals."
69   "Live Longer, Healthier like This 120-Year-Old Varanasi Monk in 5 Easy Steps."
70   Russo, Santarelli, and O'Rourke, "The Physiological Effects of Slow Breathing in the Healthy Human."

Buddhism

"The view of the Immortality of Man which I have the privilege of stating is, broadly speaking, that of the Buddhist religion."
William Sturgis Bigelow

Buddhism is controversial if reviewed among other beliefs for it lacks some common characteristics of most major religions. At its core, Buddhist school of thought preaches the capability of achieving God-like attributes, such as immortality and omniscience, while also lacks a ruler god that must be served, pleased or praised. Instead, they have Siddhartha Gautama, "The Buddha", a central figure of a man that reached the Nirvana and shared his teachings to his followers[71].

The perception of immortality for the Buddhist belief, encourages us to consider immortality as a goal to be achieved with the *elevation* of the soul to higher planes, initiating existence as simple creatures, who after dying reincarnate into more complex beings, until reaching Nirvana.

This process is described in the Tripitaka, the sacred canon of Theravada Buddhism, where the 7 main Buddhist teachings:

1. The Four Noble Truths.
2. The Noble Eightfold Path.
3. No killing. Respect for life.
4. No stealing. Respect for others' property.
5. No sexual misconduct. Respect for our pure nature.
6. No lying. Respect for honesty.
7. No intoxicants. Respect for a clear mind.

Said principles, that the Buddha came to understand during his meditation under the bodhi tree, are necessary to *elevate* the soul.

"The ultimate object of life, is to acquire freedom from the limitations of the material world by substituting volitional for sensory consciousness"[72].

---

71   Bigelow, *Buddhism and Immortality.*
72   Hollands, "Review of Buddhism and Immortality."

Chapter Seventeen

Interpretation of Religious Faith in the Roman Catholic Church

I n the Roman Catholic Church, immortality means the freedom of decay and disintegration, and thus, the freedom of death. Absolute immortality is preserved for God alone, who has no body and the spirit is of essence. For Catholics, immortality represents the doctrine that the human soul will survive death in an endless conscious existence for the individual. Moreover, the key point of any faith and the essential argument for Christianity in general and Catholicism in particular is the concept of salvation, which is interpreted as the ultimate path to eternal life with God, which his given through the life, death and resurrection of Jesus Christ for the forgiveness of all human sin leading to the escape form eternal punishment and salvation in eternity. This represents ultimate immortality of the individual, which is supposed to include his or her individuality, consciousness, character, soul and body.

In strict contrast to traditional Church teachings, the late Pope John Paul II stated in 2000 that everyone who lives a just life will be saved, even if they do not believe in Jesus Christ or the Roman Catholic Church (Los

Angeles Times, Dec 9, 2000). [73] Salvation in a sense, therefore, is leading to ever-lasting life - to immortality.

The human desire for salvation is inherent in the human nature. According to Ernest Becker, what drives human activity is purely the fear of death[74], while others like Sebastian Moore believe that human nature must contain an inert desire for life.[75]

One could argue that the driving force for all human activity is based on our inheriting goal for continuous existence. Eating, drinking, being sexually active are instinctive biologic natural processes for human (and animal) beings in order to stay alive. Similarly, carrying for offspring serves the desire to keep them alive in order to continue the traits. Practicing medicine also serves to keep the human being alive in this world. If there would be a conscious knowledge of everlasting existence or immortality in our earthly life, then why would anyone try to achieve anything, since life would be guaranteed anyhow?

The unknown, the fear of change and death, the missing promise of whatever can come to us in a future, the lust of life and joy of our earthly interactions in the world altogether and the universal desire for more than the present in our daily lives accumulate in the search for the unexplainable, the salvation beyond comprehension, and the quest for immortality.

In a Christian sense, God has created man as such with a conscious desire. Therefore, the quest for immortality can be seen on one hand as a biologic or natural instinct for survival, on the other hand as a divine creation for humankind, and also as a conscious choice based on the knowledge of human and biologic limitation with a finite life span.

---

73   Facebook et al., "Pope Takes Inclusive View of Salvation."
74   ThriftBooks, "The Denial Of Death Book by Ernest Becker."
75   "Reflexions on Death - Sebastian Moore, 1952."

Chapter Eighteen

The View of Church Fathers and Catholic Theologians

The Catholic Church fathers as well as many well-known theologians have in some way commented on immortality. Augustine of Hippo, one of the greatest Church fathers, stated that the soul is a composite of two substances, the body and the soul, and man is composed of these two things in one unity. [76]

At the time of the bodily death, however, the soul is separated and survives the death, remains alive until it will be re-united with the body at the time of the resurrection. Therefore, according to Saint Augustine, the soul as the principle of life (not death), cannot die, and is immortal. Moreover, he argues that mathematics and logic reside in the soul, and since the truth of mathematics and logic are ternal, the soul must be eternal. He also stated that the "aspiration to eternity is ontologically rooted in the essence of the human soul", which God created, and God would not have created the impossible, therefore, the soul must be immortal. [77]

---

76   Augustine, *The Confessions of St. Augustine*.
77   "Brian Brinzan, The Theory of the Immortality of the Soul with Saint Augustine, the Scientific Journal of Humanistic Studies 5, No 9 (2013), 146."

According to Thomas Aquinus, physical death does not destroy the soul, therefore the soul is incorruptible, which many argue as similar to being immortal, even though there might be a difference between the two, according to the interpretation by Linda Farmer.[78] The soul alone, however, is not the person, and therefore, the resurrection of the human body is essential for salvation rather than a continuous existence of the soul alone (Stanford Encyclopedia of Philosophy, revised 2014).[79,80]

Even though death is universal according to the early Christian author Tertullian (155-220 AD), he and others do not see death as a natural thing, but instead as a violation of nature. Death is the complete separation of body and soul, where the souls of all men after death remain in a "lower world" before the good ones re-unite with the body in resurrection (Eschatology, Tertullian.org).[81]

Modern Catholic theologians have written on the doctrine of immortality, which resembles the immortality of the soul. Catholic tradition considers immortality of the soul as a doctrine of faith, supported by the Scripture.[82]

As stated more in details above, escatology deals with the end, the end of the world, the final events

in history, and the end of humanity. Individual or personal eschatology, however, deals with the end of life and the state of the soul after death, rather than with an afterlife of the bodily individual.

Joseph Kardinal Ratzinger (born 1927), later Pope Benedict XVI, one of the most prolific and most academic theologians of the 20th century, states that according to Scripture that when man dies, "he perishes, body and soul". Furthermore, Ecclesiastes 12:7 states "then shall the dust return to earth as it was; and the spirit shall return to God who gave it", Ezekiel 18:4: *"...the soul who sins shall die"*. Ratzinger argues that *"the resurrection of the dead deals with the whole human being, and between death and resurrection, the church affirms the continuity and independent existence of the spiritual element in man after death, which we call soul"* (Kasonde, Joesph Ratzinger's reflection on the Immortality of the Soul).[83]

---

78   Farmer, "Straining the Limits of Philosophy."
79   McInerny and O'Callaghan, "Saint Thomas Aquinas."
80   Murphy, "Immortality versus Resurrection in the Christian Tradition."
81   "R.E. Roberts, The Theology of Tertullian (1924), Chapter 11 (Pp.203-218)."
82   Buchen, "The Ordeal of Richard Feverel."
83   Kasonde, "Joseph Ratzinger's Reflection on The Immortality of the Soul."

Moreover, the Catechism of the Catholic Church states: that "Spirit signifies that from creation man is ordered to a supernatural thing end and that his soul can gratuitously be raised beyond all it deserves to communion with God".[84]

Karl Rahner (1904-1984), another influential Jesuit priest and Catholic theologian of the 20th century, stated that "*the reality of man...is not abolished in death, but rather is transposed into another mode of existence*".[85] The reasoning for this thought is the idea that our human existence on earth cannot just end in nothing meaningful like cessation of biology, which he calls "the absolute null point" and the "absurd arch-contradiction of existence".[86]

For Rahner, the death of the physical body questions the meaning of life as a whole, if nothing than the decay of the body is the final result.[87]

Physical death in this context means the cessation of biochemical pathways, cellular growth and division, metabolic activity, and neuron and muscular activity as well as a complete stop of all sensory function including thoughts and dreams.

The soul therefore, does not require brain activity to continue. According to Rahner, there is a linear continuity of human temporality beyond death, where time is the process of becoming while eternity is that of being, which represents an active presence as destined human fulfillment with a "*loving immediacy to the ultimate mystery of existence called God...with limitless knowledge, love and happiness*"[88,89], or as the Swiss Catholic theologian Hans Urs von Balthazar (1905-1988) described, "*the world's ultimate destiny- as nature and as the history of mankind – is summed up both really and symbolically in the historical destiny of the man Jesus Christ...on the other side of death he begins his immortal life*"[90].

Furthermore, Rahner also stated that we do not know if a Christian really does hope for eternal life, or uses this hope "*as an analgesic so as to conceal an ultimate despair*".[91]

---

84   Church, *Catechism of the Catholic Church*.
85   "Foundations of Christian Faith."
86   ThriftBooks, "Theological Investigations V22 Book by Karl Rahner."
87   King and Whitney, "Rahner and Hartshorne on Death and Eternal Life."
88   ThriftBooks, "Theological Investigations V22 Book by Karl Rahner."
89   King and Whitney, "Rahner and Hartshorne on Death and Eternal Life."
90   Balthasar, "Easter."
91   Rahner, *The Content of Faith*.

The Swiss Catholic theologian Hans Kueng (1928-2021) who's popularity has been increased by being very critical of the Vatican, likely raised more questions than providing answers in his book "Eternal Life: Life after death as a Medical, Philosophical and Theological Problem", which resembles the unexplainability, mystery and hope leading to an enormous amount of publications on anthropological and philosophical immortality, especially of the soul.[92]

Despite a vast amount of theologic and philosophic publications and viewpoints on this topic, the mystery of faith in an eternal life remains as unbreakable as the mystery of immortality itself.

92   ThriftBooks, "Eternal Life?"

Chapter Nineteen

Remaining Questions for Christians

From a religious point of view, especially for Christians, the following questions remain open and unanswered:

1. Is it wrong to aim for immortality?
2. Is it wrong to aim for prolongation of our earthly life?
3. Is the anticipation and knowledge of the end of our earthly existence the drive which makes us live, ambitious, active, researching, wishing, dreaming, and building legacies?
4. Is it against Christian beliefs to seek biologic or bodily immortality?
5. Is bodily immortality biologically possible?
6. Are advances in technology in seeking bodily immortality replacing faith in any higher power or faith in God?
7. How does the quest for immortality affect health care providers dealing with patients with chronic diseases and end-of-life care?

Chapter Twenty

The Quest for Immortality

The search for immortality is as old as humanity and continues to be a topic of major interest for almost everyone in this world. Health-care providers are facing more and more challenges by quests form patients and caregivers to provide maximal care to prolong lives.

Immortality or even prolongation of life naturally would result in becoming older and with increased age, morbidity usually will increase, mainly secondary to degenerative changes in our tissues. Morbidity then can result in immobility, frailty, reduced quality of life, enormous health care costs, and pain and suffering.

On the other hand, however, life extension could be allied with a reasonable quality of life even at advanced ages as long as personal, social, medical, and economic support systems are made available to "compress morbidity" in the elderly.[93]

Despite the immortality quest form patients, family members and caregivers, there are countless futile cases of individuals at end-of life scenarios with incurable illnesses without any therapeutic treatment options rather than symptomatic supportive or comfort care measures. Physicians and

---

93   Faria, "Longevity and Compression of Morbidity from a Neuroscience Perspective."

nurses must embrace their limitations in providing life prolonging measures if they do not result in a meaningful and qualitative continuation of existence.[94] Therefore, mortality of the human being as part of the natural life needs to be continued to be accepted rather than concealed, by both patients as well as by health care providers. As stated above, the involvement of bioethics in certain cases might be helpful in providing guidance for healthcare providers and also for patients and families.

If our earthly live ends up in decay and disintegration, the sense of our existence has been questioned by philosophers and theologians since centuries. If all men end up in salvation through resurrection after death with an eternal life next to the divine, why then bother to seek earthly and bodily immortality in this life? Maybe, because we just do not know, maybe we are afraid of what might be coming, and maybe, because we just want to hang on to what we are used to have and to be, rather than ending up in the unknown of paradise - or hell.

Religion is helpful as *"opium for the people"* according to the German philosopher and economist Karl Marx (1818-1883) because it provides hope and brings sense and community to many lives.[95] Christianity is based on the believe in an everlasting life as a reward for living a just existence and believing in Jesus Christ as the one forgiving mortal sin and providing life in eternity in a divine sphere.

The yearning for immortality has been the subject of a University of California investigation called the "Immortality Research Project" which included different scientific disciplines from philosophy to biology to religion to evaluate immortality as published in "The Science of Immortality" by Michael Cholbi in 2018.[96] If immortality is in reach and biologically feasible secondary to genetic manipulation of the processes of aging and appropriate repair mechanisms in regenerative medicine, does this render faith in the resurrection and in an afterlife obsolete just based on lack of necessity? In other words, does modern biotechnology replace not only religious beliefs but even Christianity, Judaism and Islam as a whole?

---

94   Macmillan and Geraci, "Culture Shift."
95   Pedersen, "RELIGION IS THE OPIUM OF THE PEOPLE."
96   Cholbi, "Immortality Project Research Review."

In our opinion, the answer is no, for the following reasons:

1. Biology is not able to replace faith as a way of life and living, as a guide through hard times, as something giving hope for all believers.

2. Computed technology does not replace human consciousness, thoughts, abstract thinking, reasoning, conscious decision making, or emotional feeling such as happiness, grief, hope or love.

3. Science is able to explain how things work but fails to explain why things happen.

4. Science is limited in its ability to explain the unknown and the unexplainable.

5. Science is constantly changing while faith remains over thousands of years.

6. Christian faith and the Catholic Church as well as most other religions do accept modern sciences including Darwin's theory of the evolution.

7. Biblical writings are meant to be understood symbolically rather than factually.

8. Biotechnology advances in techniques to replace degenerated tissues and to halt processes of aging, which will result in a prolongation of life.

9. Complete biologic immortality for the human beings on earth will not be achievable within a foreseeable future.

10. Healthcare providers dealing with the very sick need to provide ethical judgement on end-of life care decisions not based on futuristic fictious visions for immortality but based on human integrities, righteousness and medical possibilities and impossibilities for humane end-of life therapy and death.

Chapter Twenty-One

Different Types of Immortality

I n order to understand what immortality for the human being means, one needs to distinguish the term immortality and differentiate in a systematic manner. We took the liberty based on published data but also on our own studies to create a list of the different types of immortality which does not claim to be all-inclusive.

As such, let us evaluate first what we might call *natural immortality*.

Natural immortality is found in a Jelly fish that endlessly replicate, even after external damage and does lack signs of aging and degeneration. This natural immortality is the basis for several biological research projects but likely not achievable for higher differentiated organisms such as humans.

Second, let us talk about *biologic immortality*.

Biologic immortality we would call a biologically defined extended life span, such as the life span of certain sharks or whales reaching up to a few hundred years. This biologic immortality should be considered more as a prolongation of life by means of modern medicine and technology to combat disease such as heart and vascular diseases and cancer and likely is achievable to reach human ages above 120 years within this century.

Third, *literal immortality* represents a more philosophical aspect on the topic.

Literal immortality is considered a metaphysical concept, meaning that the human nature is not automatically destroyed by death but may exist forever (in whatever sphere).

Fourth, **symbolic immortality** deals with the conception of continued existence of the human or his legacies, work, thoughts and so on, as he/she can be remembered by living individuals such as friends or family members or disciples or fans or the society.

Fifth, **spiritual immortality** is what we would call the immortality of the soul, either eternal, or temporarily before rejoining the body according to the resurrection, or even independent on any symbiosis with a body in a space apart from or beyond our earthly existence.

Sixth, **supernatural immortality** is divine or religious immortality, based on religious faith as in Christianity (or in other religions), the resurrection of the individual after death in body and soul in a different sphere such as heaven or in any realm close to divinity.

Seventh, **digital immortality** is the currently developed technology that enables us to conserve everything that is known about a human being in digital form, whether it is his or her knowledge, character, mood swings, experiences, or personal traits so that anyone could then virtually communicate and talk to Jesus Christ or Albert Einstein or deceased family members via a computer, as examples. Technology obviously has advanced accordingly and this kind of preservation of a person's individuality in a downloaded electric version is already in progress.

Another distinguishing factor between the above types of immortality can be the separation of eternal life dependent on its location, whether on earth (such as biologic immorality) or somewhere else (such as spiritual immortality).

The current facts of the above types of immortality are as follows:

1. Natural immortality is existent in some species, is the basis for basic research to evaluate the biochemical pathways and processes of aging and genetic manipulation of senescence. The expectations

are that natural immortality might translate to biologic immortality within the next 100 years.

2. Biologic immortality is the basis for medical therapy, disease management and pre-clinical and clinical research in order to survive certain disease, and prolong life, is currently existent and rapidly progressing as a result of pharmacologic and therapeutic interventions. Expectations are that biologic immortality will prolong life above 120 years of age, even 150 years or more within the next 50 years.

3. Literal immortality and spiritual immortality will remain a concept for philosophy, religion and theology.

4. Symbolic immortality is a continuum dependent on anyone's legacy, whether it is a development of a theory, the creation of a smartphone, or a gesture to a family which does not require more than an individual's goals in life.

5. Spiritual immortality or the immortality of the soul remains a philosophical concept and a concept of faith. Certain reports on near death experiences have argued for the existence of spiritual immortality.

6. Supernatural immortality or divine immortality remains the basis for religious beliefs, in Christian theology, the resurrection after death represents the ultimate divine salvation.

7. Digital immortality is based on technology alone, is currently under development and obviously practically achievable within the next 10 years.

Chapter Twenty-Two

Attempt to Answer Questions on Immortality from a Roman Catholic View

I mmortality of the soul is not a Christian thought that is taught and is not an official doctrine of the Catholic Church. According to Oscar Cullman, the idea of the immortality of the soul "is one of the greatest misunderstandings of Christianity"[97]. Moreover, immortality itself as a term is not something the Catholic Church likes to use but instead, the teachings prefer to deal with the resurrection after death and everlasting or eternal life (Ratzinger, Eschatology, Death and Eternal Life, 1988).[98] The Scripture clearly says "he perishes, body and soul", which prompted Ratzinger to state that "Only in this fashion can one preserve the idea of death as a judgement", and therefore, traditional Catholic teachings prefer the resurrection of the complete human being.

Some theologians have addressed the issue of the dilemma of the explanations between the sciences on whatever might happen after death. Of interest, in the German language sciences are categorized between "Natur-

---

97   Cullmann, *Immortality of the Soul or Resurrection of the Dead?*
98   *Eschatology.*

wissenschaften", which equals natural sciences such as biology, physics, chemistry and so on, and "Geisteswissenschaften" (Geist is translated as ghost, or spirit or mind), which content the sciences of theory, such as philosophy, theology, Germanistics, and so on. In view of becoming more aware of the natural processes of the developmental character of our world, there are "...*extremely profound problems of a "harmonization" of the theological data and our natural knowledge of the world*".[99] In other words, there is the growing and ever more apparent discrepancy of old-school traditional but "altmodisch" (German, = old fashioned) (Catholic Church) teaching rituals and the populistic and widespread awareness of the scientific explanations of the beginning of the world and the development of species from single cells to the homo sapiens. While natural science can explain all these molecular processes in all details, meaning the *how* is deeply investigated, the *why* remains unanswered and remains only explainable but the higher power, or God. While the tree in front of us can be explained in all its microstructural elements by biology and chemistry, the horizon behind the tree is always there, no matter where we go, which resembles God as the horizon in our world, according to Karl Rahner.[100]

Is death bad? Of course, in our view, death is the final cessation of life in this world, and therefore, must be bad. Death leads to non-existence, almost similar to non-existence before we are born. Without birth and before birth, we are non-existent. Even though, we humans naturally do not care much about nonexistence before birth, we do care about nonexistence after our earthly life.

Death therefore can be seen as evil, since it disrupts all our activities, dreams and plans. According to Scripture, death is also the result of sin, but the gift of God is eternal life in Christ (Romans 6:23). But death is not always related to the devil or Satan, since death is somehow a natural process, and only God can provide eternal life through salvation and resurrection after death. As natural as death is as part of life, so is the quest for eternal life, among all cultures, all epochs, and in all religions.

---

99   Rahner, *The Content of Faith*.
100   Rahner, *Theological Investigations Volume IV*.

Death is considered a bad thing, since it ends everything we know for us and the people around us. Death is final with regard to its abrupt cessation of having a person in his /her entirety with us. Death is the horrible cessation of all we know, and the expectations of eternal life for Christians have not much in common with the radical turning point death creates for every human being as clearly depicted in a lecture given by Karl Rahner, *Erfahrungen eines katholischen Theologen*, at a festivity for his 80th birthday in 1984.[101]

Death is sometimes considered like sleep, but sleep is not death, and our bodily functions are active during sleep, in contrast to no functions in death. On the other hand, death is the end, the non-existence of the human being, similar to a non-existence before birth.

According to Ratzinger, the crucial denominator of life or death is nothing else but just time.[102] Existence in a future life therefore must be independent on time as we know it and beyond time on order to be immortal. Mikel Burley argues that eternal life for Christians should be seen in the context of four dimensionalist metaphysics in which parts of time are as real as parts of space, with past, present and future are real and exist eternally.[103]

---

101 "Von Der Unbegreiflichkeit Gottes. Erfahrungen Eines Katholischen Theologen Geisteswissenschaften Religion Theologie Christentum Glaube Philosophie Christliche Religionen Rahner, Karl Theologe Karl Rahner, Albert Raffelt Und Karl Lehmann Herder Verlag Erstmals Als Buchveröffentlichung Karl Rahners Letzte Große Rede. In Seinen 'Erfahrungen Eines Theologen' Fasst Karl Rahner Die Anleigen Seines Theologischen Lebens Zusammen Und Lässt Zugleich in Sein Herz Blickenein Geistliches Testament Für Das 21. Jahrhundert. Autor Karl Rahner SJ, 1904 -1984; Lehrtätigkeit in Innsbruck, München Und Münster. Er Ist Einer Der Bedeutenden Theologen Des 20.Jahrhunderts Und Ein Großer Spiritueller Lehrer. Albert Raffelt, Dr. Theol., Geb. 1944, Ist Bibliotheksdirektor a. D. Und Honorarprofessor Für Dogmatische Theologie an Der Universität Freiburg i. Br.Prof. Dr. Phil. Dr. Theol. Karl Kardinal Lehmann, Geboren 1936, Ist Bischof von Mainz Und War von 1987 Bis 2008 Vorsitzender Der Deutschen Bischofskonferenz. by Karl Rahner Dr. Theol. Albert Raffelt Bibliotheksdirektor a. D. Honorarprofessor Für Dogmatische Theologie Universität Freiburg i. Br. Prof. Dr. Phil. Dr. Theol. Karl Kardinal Lehmann."

102 *Eschatology.*

103 Burley, "Immortality and Meaning."

Chapter Twenty-Three

Is Immortality Desirable?

The question is, however, if mankind can achieve biologic immortality, whether this immortality would be a gift or a curse. Whether or not, however, immortality is desirable, is another question.

According to John Martin Fischer there are three required characteristics that would make immortality worth the efforts for the individual human being to search for:[104]

1. Identification, i.e., the continuous existence of the individual without evolving into a different person, even in a million years from now despite evolution of the world around us;

2. Attractiveness, i.e., the immortal life has to be desirable due to its quality, rather than a prolonged or everlasting degeneration and decay which would not render any joy and happiness;

3. Recognizability, i.e., the immortal person has to be the one who seeks immortality from the get go, rather than someone who changes over time and loses his/her character, identity, personality or memories in its original senses.

---

104   Fischer, "Immortality."

In its purest sense, this would mean biologic immortality or possibly spiritual immortality rather than a transhumanistic alteration between the individuals traits and computer technology.

On one hand we aim for an immortal life that should be somewhat similar to our current life with identification, attractiveness, and recognizability. On the other hand, a life in a different universe outside time might represent a distinct deviation for our current existence, as it might be in heaven in a divine realm. Such an immortal existence remains unexplainable by means of our current natural sciences and beyond our intellectual and technological understanding and capabilities.

Assuming that natural sciences might be able to create biologic immortality on this earth, again, it remains questionable whether the infinite duration of life might then change the sense, contour and destination of human existence, "with no meaningful differentiation between climaxes".[105] Moreover, if we would live forever, how would the infinite existence change our behaviors, why having morals or ethical questions if nothing ever could happen to us, why seeking, studying and researching for anything if we are staying alive in any case. Would all our ambition, our interpersonal relationships, our dependencies, our values, trust, our beliefs be in vain since nothing would lead to anything more than what has be defined as infinite already? Is not the awareness and unchangeable defined end what drives us today, to build a family, a relationship until death do us apart, a legacy to live on in the memories of our children, friends, or fans? Fischer and Mitchell-Yellin argue against the boredom of immortality and state that an immortal life could bring never-ending new experiences and pleasures that might never be boring.[106]

Or, on the other hand, if biologic immortality will be achieved, will that mean then that we might exist as a jelly fish creature, a jelly fish that lives forever, but besides this, the author cannot imagine much excitement of being like a jelly fish, life's anticipation, momentum and appeal might be exchanged to boredom and a stoic living existence instead (the author asks

---

105   May, *Death*.
106   Fischer and Mitchell-Yellin, "Immortality and Boredom."

humbly for forgiveness to insulted a jelly fish species since I might not be able to understand the jelly fish's real fun in life).

But again, immortality can be a curse, too. There is the story of the wandering Jew, who supposedly taunted Jesus on the way to his crucifixion and then was cursed by Jesus to life forever[107].

According to Eugene Fontinell any believe in immortality is justified only if the immortal state would enhance life to a different or better level, not just a continuation of the current existence[108]. Even the German philosopher Nietsche despite his attacks on standard religion, considers a future of humankind with a life more creative and fulfilling. Nietsche states in his *Gay Science* to consider if a demon makes man lives the same life over and over again that this would be a disaster and nothing to wish for, unless one would be able to embrace life on earth as an absolute pleasure (which would be the role of the "Uebermensch").[109] Moreover, according to Adam Buben, Nietsche stated that "very few of us would be worth preserving, despite what the democratic impulses of Christianity have to say. The vast majority of humans are not particularly impressive or interesting insofar as we just propagate traditional values uncritically, and there is little reason to believe we would do anything differently if we had more time".[110] While Nietsche embraces the eternal recurrence in this life, Christianity usually sees our current earthly existence as inferior to the one coming after the resurrection which is a better life in paradise.[111]

The curse could be not to know what to do with all your time unless immortality or at least an increased health span would ensure a healthy and productive life until very high ages. Socioeconomically, this could otherwise create a major problem. Is it against Christian belief to seek bodily immortality? Would this replace resurrection, and conditional immortality? In a sense, it might. On the other hand, it is a pre-requisite of Christian faith to strongly belief in immortality, which resembles the base for the religion (and

---

107   *The Legend of the Wandering Jew.*
108   Fontinell, "Immortality," 2000.
109   Nietzsche, *The Gay Science.*
110   Buben, "The Dark Side of Desire."
111   Buben.

is natural for Christians in that sense) as well as the kingdom for humanity to come.[112] The lack of evidence does not defy its strong role in Christian faith. Again, in this sense, immortality is not defined but usually is related to resurrection with an ever-lasting life - as a result of Christian faith.

In a sense of realism, one must consider that life is terminal, and whether or not an afterlife exists, even embarrasses theologians, according to Hans Kueng, "Ich glaube nicht an ein endloses Leben auf dieser Erde. Aber ich glaube an ein ewiges Leben ... Das heißt: Ich möchte ... nicht eine unbeschränkte Verlängerung des irdischen Lebens in Zeit und Raum. Ich hoffe auf ein ... vollkommen verwandeltes Leben in Gottes Ewigkeit"[113]. Like Kueng, who has been heavily criticized for his view especially on the Catholic church and the papal infallibility, many do not seek everlasting existence on earth or a prolongation of the current life with all its issues including waning health, reduction in function and capabilities, developing dementia and social burdens but in an afterlife beyond the sphere of our understanding. Most philosophers but also theologians believe that the earthly life is terminal, and death is final. The irony of immortality could be that man's efforts to extending his earthly life on a physical plane might prevent man from existing with the source of all creation in a heavenly paradise.

On the other hand, in a Christian view, resurrection of the death does not automatically guarantee personal survival after death.[114]

---

112 Buben.
113 Küng, *Ewiges Leben?*
114 Fontinell, "Immortality," 2000.

Chapter Twenty-Four

Populistic Considerations on Immortality

I s immortality biologically possible in this day and age?

"The person who will live a 1000 years is already born" was a statement from the documentary *Immortals* in 2018. Of interest, longevity is supposedly determined only 20% by genetics, the remainder is determined by lifestyle, diseases, medical therapy and the environment.

In the introduction of his popular book "Immortality Inc.", Chip Walter quotes a New York Times opinion writer stating that the search for immortality is "inhuman" and that "death is a blessing. It gives life meaning.[115]

In 2013, the tech company Calico was founded in Silicon Valley, largely funded by Google, to tackle aging ("google versus death", Time Magazine).[116] Then Human Longevity, Inc., followed a year later with the goal of extending a high-performance human life span.

Alcor, a cryo preservation company that keeps the bodies of deceased individuals frozen in Scottsdale, Arizona advertises its service with the slogan "absolute death versus a shot at resurrection". Cryopreservation is a well

---

115   Walter, *Immortality, Inc.*
116   "Google vs. Death."

established and widely used method since over 30 years originating from in vitro fertilization to preserve sperm or fertilized oocytes for years prior to bring them back to live at any time later.[117] Cryopreservation of people who died is a relatively new trend that created business worldwide to preserve the bodies after earthly death.[118]

Cryopreservation by creating "cryonauts" who are dead but vitrified, however, with a pre- death dated hope to be re-animated or re-vitalized at a time when medicine and science is advanced enough to resuscitate the thawed dead bodies and re-institute life, is not creating immortality, is not prolonging life at this time, and is not providing any anti-aging technologies.

In contrast, biotechnologies and medicine's goal is to avoid (or at least delay) decrepitude and death.

Immortality therefore, in a populistic sense, is closely related to aging and anti-aging. The science of gerontology deals with the issues of aging, the science of geriatrics deals with age-related loss of function, mobility, independence, and diseases of the elderly. Aging research on the other hand, attempts to study the biological processes of aging and the options to delay or prevent aging and cell death.

Of interest, however, the only one condition that is capable to stop aging is - death. With death, aging stops, indefinitely.

In that sense, death is the one and only current anti-aging solution. And death, even in a religious sense, is final - at least until the resurrection.

Most cultures deal with death in a morbid fascination, in art, music, and daily life. As an example, Austria's capital Vienna has had historically the death theme all over its history and culture up until this day, from the acceptance of popular songs ("Wenn der Herrgott nit will, nuetzt des garnix" = if God does not want, it doesn't matter, by Hans Moser in the 1950s) to the celebration of its main cemetery ("Es lebe der Zentralfriedhof" = long live the central cemetery, by Wolfgang Ambros in the 1980s).

However, since big corporations like Google and Apple threw their smartest minds and a lot of money into anti-aging companies such as Calico

---

117   Trounson, "Cryopreservation."2-propanediol (PROH
118   Mayor, "Sixty Seconds on . . . Cryopreservation."

and Human Longevity, Inc., among others, the search defying aging and death suddenly became not only scientific and scientifically reputable but also technologically plausible, even within our lifetime.

Google, Apple and other Silicon Valley corporations ultimate goal was and still is: to kill death. That particular prospect is just what the baby boomer generation (who are currently in their 50s-60s) wants to hear. It created an outburst of biotechnology companies to appear (such as SENS Research Foundation, Stemcentrx, United Therapeutics, among many others) with the common goal to gain longevity and immortality. More recently, it was also announced that both Jeff Bezos, CEO of AMAZON and considered the richest man in the world, together with a Russian billionaire, funded a new Silicon Valley company named Altos Labs which also is supposed to reverse processes of aging.

As stated earlier in our systematic differentiation on immortality, from a populistic view, the main types of immortality that are of public interest are natural, biological and digital immortality (rather than spiritual or divine immortality). There is a substantial difference between natural and biological immortality, and digital immortality. Digital immortality is the use of technology to preserve an individual's memory personality in a digital (computerized) medium, which is in reach due to technological advances. Natural immortality - according to our definition - in contrast, is the never-ending existence of a biological system, body or individual, which would require genetic manipulation of the processes of senescence beyond what is feasible at the current time. Biologic immortality is what we attempt using modern medicine and technology to improve outcomes and to prolong life.

Chapter Twenty-Five

The Medical Perspective on Immortality

Primum non nocere

The medical sciences exist as a natural consequence of humanity's search to preserve life and health. One of the most fascinating vestiges of civilization resides in the remains of a hominid with data on a healed femur fracture.[119] We distinguish ourselves by caring to heal the wounded, help the needy and live together in society. The structure of our intellect as well as scientific and technological advances led us to systematize our practices, establish codes and treaties to define good practice in any discipline.

The Hippocratic Oath, written between the fifth and third centuries BC, and its subsequent updates incite to "utmost respect for human life from its beginning", beginning with the "*Primum non nocere*" (first, do no harm), adapted in its lines from the seventeenth century.[120] This oath is taken by physicians around the world and encourages us to preserve life and its quality, which aligns with the concept of delaying aging and pursuing immortality.

119   Blumenfeld, "How A 15,000-Year-Old Human Bone Could Help You Through The Coronacrisis."
120   "Greek Medicine - The Hippocratic Oath."

The concept of "health span", meaning prolonging life in regards to quality of years lived rather than just surviving the years left to live, is stressed through various physiological parameters as described below. [121]

There are some new data available regarding life-style changes, medications and procedures that might be able to support prolongation of health and even life. As an example, calorie restriction before the onset of old age, i.e., before the age of 60 years, could delay aging through various negative/positive feedback mechanisms, thereby delaying cardiovascular aging, decreasing the risk of cancer and other metabolic disorders, enhancing the quality of life, and leading to longevity.[122]

In addition, there are reports of certain medications such as Metformin, a diabetes drug, and Rapamycin, an antifungal antibiotic drug, which potentially can be considered as having anti-aging (and also anti-cancer) properties with documented evidence of prolongation of life, a phenomenon that is called "geroconversion". Animal studies suggest that consuming these medications prior to the onset of illness could exhibit benefits on the delay of processes of aging.[123]

Some anti-aging remedies have shown to improve quality of life and to prolonging lifespan, however, no large scale controlled randomized trials are available to support these hypotheses.[124]

Implementing life-style modification and adapting to a primordial prevention system while decreasing risk factors could theoretically reduce cardiac death by 90% and even might prolong life-expectancy by ten or more years, according to some authors.[125] Furthermore, appropriate psychological, nutritional, and social/family support could extend the longevity in general, as evidenced by the frequently quoted "blue-zone" findings.[126] Blue zones represent areas in different geographic locations all over the world from Japan to Greece to California with a very high longevity. Common denominators within these blue zones have been a healthy, balanced, plant-based

121   van Beek, Kirkwood, and Bassingthwaighte, "Understanding the Physiology of the Ageing Individual."
122   Eissenberg, "Hungering for Immortality."
123   Blagosklonny, "Rapamycin for Longevity."
124   Blagosklonny, "How to Save Medicare."
125   Mishra, "Does Modern Medicine Increase Life-Expectancy."
126   Buettner and Skemp, "Blue Zones."

diet, physical activity, and an active social participation within the living communities until high ages.

Certain plant-based supplements such as adaptogens, bacopa monnieri, curcuma longa, emblica officinalis, ginkgo biloba, glycyrrhiza glabra, and panax ginseng as well as metabolites such as certain polyphenols, carotenoids, vitamins C and E do possess some anti-inflammatory, antioxidant, and anticancer properties.[127] These properties could contribute to delay aging and to prolong life, to some extent.

---

127 Dhanjal et al., "Plant Fortification of the Diet for Anti-Ageing Effects."

Chapter Twenty-Six

Inflammaging

The concept of *"inflammaging"* is a new dimension in research that is yet to be established as an age-related phenomenon. [128] It is described as a condition that accompanies aging through an ongoing inflammatory process, ultimately resulting in a reduction in immunity and exhausting the body's defense system. Recent studies using mesenchymal stem cell therapy have shown promising results on immunomodulation to a disease-free state properties by means of tissue antiinflammation and tissue regeneration, supporting the concept of inflammaging processes. [129] The use of pluripotent stem cells demonstrated growth properties and tissue development similar to properties of embryonic stem cells, as evidenced by the detection of marker genes. [130]

128   Sanada et al., "Source of Chronic Inflammation in Aging."
129   Lee and Yu, "Impact of Mesenchymal Stem Cell Senescence on Inflammaging."
130   Takahashi and Yamanaka, "Induction of Pluripotent Stem Cells from Mouse Embryonic and Adult Fibroblast Cultures by Defined Factors."

Chapter Twenty-Seven

Gene Reprogramming

Others are reprograming cells to develop into any tissue types. Genetic *reprogramming* also attempts to manipulate genes responsible for cellular senescence in order to completely avoid the processes of aging.[131]

Reprogramming is a biologic technique that involves de-differentiation of adult somatic cells to produce patient-specific pluripotent stem cells to be used for therapeutic reasons. The ideal cell types from a biologic point of view would be embryonic cells since these cells have the most potent power (good enough to create an entire human body), but the use of embryonic cells or even to produce embryos for research purposes is not only unethical but also not allowed in most countries.

Reprogramming factors may remodel the epigenetic code of differentiated cells to one resembling epigenetic code. Pluripotency genes are activated and differentiation genes are muted. Epigenetic reprogramming occurs during gametogenesis and the preimplantation embryonic period. Reprogramming during gametogenesis is necessary for the imprinting mechanism that regulates the differential expression of maternally and paternally derived genes.

---

131   Romito and Cobellis, "Pluripotent Stem Cells."

Induced pluripotent stem cells are a special form of manipulated cells that are derived from differentiated adult cells through genetic programming, are not only theoretically able to generate unlimited numbers of cells but also it bypasses the issues of allogeneic immune rejection. Induced pluripotent stem cells can be used to turn any cell of the body into a stem cell. However, there are many unanswered questions using induced pluripotent stem cell outside the research laboratory including the potential of inducing tumors or cancer. Therefore, there are several ethical concerns using induced pluripotent stem cells in human at the current time, but the biologic mechanisms that enable cells to be reprogrammed could be a way to manipulate processes of senescence (cellular aging) in the near future.

Chapter Twenty-Eight

Regenerative Medicine

Regenerative medicine by use of stem cell therapy is one of the most promising advances in modern biology and medicine. It can involve the use of cellular and/or acellular products to stimulate metabolic pathways that normally tend to deteriorate with aging.[132]

Stem cell therapy is nothing new but has bene around since decades, in particular stem cell have been used for the treatment of certain forms of cancer as stem cell transplantation. This is, however, different form todays stem cell therapy, where exogenous injection of autonomous (retrieved from the patient, isolated and then re-injected) or allogenic stem cells (form donor tissue ssuch as umbilical chord blood or placenta tissue)) in patients are supposed to help to repair damage in certain organs. My research group was among the first in the world to use embryonic cells to mimic the effects of

---

132 Dzobo et al., "Advances in Regenerative Medicine and Tissue Engineering."trauma, and diseases. The human body has a low regenerative potential as opposed to the urodele amphibians commonly referred to as salamanders. Globally, millions of people would benefit immensely if tissues and organs can be replaced on demand. Traditionally, transplantation of intact tissues and organs has been the bedrock to replace damaged and diseased parts of the body. The sole reliance on transplantation has created a waiting list of people requiring donated tissues and organs, and generally, supply cannot meet the demand. The total cost to society in terms of caring for patients with failing organs and debilitating diseases is enormous. Scientists and clinicians, motivated by the need to develop safe and reliable sources of tissues and organs, have been improving therapies and technologies that can regenerate tissues and in some cases create new tissues altogether. Tissue engineering and/or regenerative medicine are fields of life science employing both engineering and biological principles to create new tissues and organs and to promote the regeneration of damaged or diseased tissues and organs. Major advances and innovations are being made in the fields of tissue engineering and regenerative medicine and have a huge impact on three-dimensional bioprinting (3D bioprinting

stem cells in experimental animal models by using embryonic hearts from pregnant rats that then were injected in recipient animals that had experimentally induced heart attacks weeks earlier. By injecting male embryonic cells into female recipients, we were able to detect the Y chromosome (male chromosome) to proof that the cells came from the cell injections. We demonstrated that the cells did survive and also improved cardiac function in those animals with prior heart attacks.[133] Adding vascular growth factor in addition to embryonic cell transplantation in these animals, further fostered functional improvement, as shown by my group.[134]

As outlined in our recent publication in details "...*results of these initial basic research animal studies created hype around the search for the clinical use of stem cells in humans with the design of several clinical trials using different kinds of stem cells for acute and chronic heart diseases as well as other devastating illnesses. Consequently, the first clinical studies using stem cell therapy in patients with heart disease were published in the year 2000 (over twenty years ago). Precursor cells derived from bone marrow were the first types of cells used in clinical studies in humans with the idea that the transplantation of healthy, multipotent cells would promote the renewal of damaged tissue, the replacement of scars, and the repair of degenerative changes in order to develop into functional cells with an improvement of function (strength) and outcomes*".[135]

Stem cell therapy represents the major aspect of regenerative medicine, in which we use cellular products that have the unique omnipotency (or pluripotency) to develop into any tissue, i.e., if injected into the heart, they can become cardiomyocytes (heart muscle cells), if injected in the liver, they can become hepatocytes (liver cells), if injected into the sin, they can become dermatocytes (skin cells). Regeneration is the goal, rather than just dealing with damage without the ability of repair, as it is done currently using standard *reactive* medicine, where we react as a result of damage rather than repairing anything.

Anti-aging is fundamentally cogitated to elicit repair.

---

133 Skobel et al., "Transplantation of Fetal Cardiomyocytes into Infarcted Rat Hearts Results in Long-Term Functional Improvement."

134 Schuh et al., "Administration of Vascular Endothelial Growth Factor Adjunctive to Fetal Cardiomyocyte Transplantation and Improvement of Cardiac Function in the Rat Model."

135 Schwarz, *The Secret World of Stem Cell Therapy.*

Chapter Twenty-Nine

Faith and Science: Towards Convergence and Harmony

"Life, which you will look for, you will never find. For when the gods created man, then let death be his share, and life withheld in their own hands". [136]

This is a quote from the oldest literature available in the world, the Epic of Gilgamesh, approximately 2100 B.C., which already dealt with the search for immortality. Similar to the monotheistic religions after Christ, faith in ancient Mesopotamia, though polytheistic, included the belief in creation and the immortality of their gods, but also in an afterlife following death to what was called the underworld, a land below our world (Irkallu). [137] Faith in monotheistic religions, as per sacred texts in Christianity, Islam and Judaism, include a life after death.

Is Faith Contradicting Science or does Science Contradict Faith?

There is a schism between theology and sciences.

---

136   *The Epic of Gilgamesh.*
137   Noegel, "GOD OF HEAVEN AND SHEOL."

Does religion oppose science? Does science contradict faith? Or both? Neurosciences never showed that there is no spiritual mind or soul. There is no intrinsic conflict between science and religion. Reason and faith are complimentary in understanding the world, the universe and our lives.

Jesuit priests on the popular website and Youtube channel Aquinas 101, Faith and Science ask: Does belief in miracles and traditional dogmas require us to deny scientific evidence, or abandon the scientific method? Not really, I guess.

Does Schroedinger's cat invalidate the principle of non-contradiction (in which contradictory propositions cannot be true in the same sense at the same time, or in other words according to Aristotle in Metaphysics: "For the same thing to be present and not be present at the same time at the same subject, and according to the same, is impossible"[138])?[139]

One of the answers to these questions, from a Catholic point of view, is that the Catholic faith does not need to fear contemporary science, at least, according to Thomas Aquinas.[140]

One of the core issues of dialogue and debate between the church and scientists since centuries has been the origin of life, species, and humanity. The Catholic Church is not against Darwin's theory of evolution. Darwin proposed the stepwise development of higher species originating from lower ones through natural selection, meaning simple organisms developed into more complicated and more specified organisms in order to adapt, compete, survive and reproduce as a response to different environmental factors.[141]

Several popes have published statements about the origin of life and somehow accept evolution, but the Catholic Church does not believe that evolution happened by itself naturalistically without the creation, induction, or guidance by God.[142]

---

138   Aristotle, *The Metaphysics.*
139   "Schrödinger's Cat."
       Schrodinger's cat is an experience that presents a paradox in which a cat in a box is simultaneously both alive and dead. In the experiment, a cat, a flask full of poison and a radioactive source are placed in a sealed box. If an internal monitor detects any radioactivity, the flask full of poison is shattered and the poison kills the cat. According to the quantum mechanics, a particle stays in all possible states until observed. This means that a thing, a molecule, an atom, or an animal can be in different conditions, at the same time. In this particular example, the cat can be and therefore is simultaneously both alive and dead, if the observer is outside the box. If someone opens the box and looks into it, however, the cat is either alive or dead (not both). At any time before opening the box, there is a 50:50 chance (50%) for the cat of being alive or dead.
140   "Aquinas 101."
141   Darwin, *The Origin of Species.*'On the Origin of Species by Means of Natural Selection, or the Preservation of Favoured Races in the Struggle for Life';
142   Wiker, *The Catholic Church & Science.*

There are many arguments against the mainstream ideas that the Catholic Church would oppose modern science in order to hold on to antique traditions. We are mentioning a few examples that might be interest in particular of interest for health care providers here.

Ezekiel 36:26 says:

> *A new heart also will I give you, and a new spirit will I put within you: and I will take away the stony heart out of your flesh, and I will give you a heart of flesh.*

Even though mostly interpreted as giving a heart of spirit rather than keeping a heart that is emotionless, many transplant cardiologists (including myself) have used this quotation more than once while talking to patients prior to planned cardiac transplantation. I addition, I have heard almost similar statements from patients with end-stage heart failure who were considered candidates for cardiac transplantation such as a German patient who said to me: "I was born with the heart my mother and my God gave me and if it is meant to be, then I will die with this heart".

Other patients I have encountered argued: "My church will not support me having a heart transplant". Both of these statements are not at all representing a Christian sense or the view of the Catholic Church.

One could argue scientifically that the quotation in Ezekiel might be interpreted as God is talking to a person with an illness called *amyloidosis* (a heart of stone), which is a condition that stiffens the heart muscle due to a deposition of certain proteins for unknown reasons and make it feel like a "heart of stone". The only "curative therapy" available is in fact to replace such a heart with a transplantation (*I will give you a heart of flesh*).

Even though the biblical writers might not have been made aware of the concept of amyloidosis since it was first described by the German physician Rudolph Virchow (1821-1902) in 1854, however, no one really knows what these writers were aware of.[143]

---

143   Sipe and Cohen, "Review."in 1854, introduced and popularized the term amyloid to denote a macroscopic tissue abnormality that exhibited a positive iodine staining reaction. Subsequent light microscopic studies with polarizing optics demonstrated the inherent birefringence of amyloid deposits, a property that increased intensely after staining with Congo

As a result of our patient's encounter, we recently have investigated the Catholic Churches view on organ (heart) transplantation, in general. Donating an organ such as a heart after brain death has occurred in fact is considered the highest level of altruism, according to a statement by the Vatican and Pope Benedict XVI, and therefore, is fully supported by the Catholic Church.[144]

In addition, it is false to believe that the Catholic Church is opposing sciences since it would contradict the ideas in the scripture about genesis origins. The widely quoted publication by William Draper entitled "history of the conflict between religion and science" from 1874, which was called the conflict thesis, is not accepted as a contradiction by the Catholic Churches on sciences today, in contrast to the view of many atheists.[145]

---

red dye. In 1959, electron microscopic examination of ultrathin sections of amyloidotic tissues revealed the presence of fibrils, indeterminate in length and, invariably, 80 to 100 A in width. Using the criteria of Congophilia and fibrillar morphology, 20 or more biochemically distinct forms of amyloid have been identified throughout the animal kingdom; each is specifically associated with a unique clinical syndrome. Fibrils, also 80 to 100 A in width, have been isolated from tissue homogenates using differential sedimentation or solubility. X-ray diffraction analysis revealed the fibrils to be ordered in the beta pleated sheet conformation, with the direction of the polypeptide backbone perpendicular to the fibril axis (cross beta structure

144   Schwarz and Rosanio, "Religion and the Catholic Church's View on (Heart) Transplantation."
145   FLEMING, *John William Draper and the Religion of Science.*

Chapter Thirty

The Interactions Between Science and Theology

There are four original models of interactions between science and religion, as outlined by Ian Barbour's *Issues in Science and Religion*, written in 1966.[146] This provided the framework for the development of the thriving inter-disciplinary world of "Science and "Religion."[147] Years later in 1991, Jonathon Brooke proposed *"the complexity thesis,"* which is now also commonly considered a fifth model of interaction between science and religion.[148,149]

146 Barbour, *Issues in Science and Religion.*
147 Barbour, *Religion and Science.*"ISBN":"978-0-06-060938-2","language":"English","number-of-pages":"3 84","publisher":"HarperOne","publisher-place":"San Francisco","source":"Amazon","title":"Religion and Science","author":[{"family":"Barbour","given":"Ian G."}],"issued":{"date-parts":[["1997",8,2]]}}}],"schema":"https://github.com/citation-style-language/schema/raw/master/csl-citation.json"}
148 Says, "Science, Religion, and Secularism Part VI."
149 Brooke, "Science, Religion, and Historical Complexity."AS THE DISHNGUISHED HISTORIAN OF scienceJohn Hedley Brooke notes, that in a time when historians are deeply suspicious of metanarratives, there has been a decidedemphasis on historicalcomplexity. Nowhere is this more evidentthan in the history of science andreligion, a subjectto which Brooke has made substantial contributions. Inplace of the warfare metaphor, historians of science andreligion have adoptedan anti-essentialist approach, dubbedthe \"complexity thesis\" and often associated with Brooke's work. Close examination ofparticular historicalcontexts does not reveal \"some timeless inherent relationship\" between science and religion. But, as Brooke and Geoffrey Cantor warned in their Gifford Fectures, preoccupation withparticular contexts might dissolve \"thegreat issues that have been debated under the banner of 'science and religion' into thefragments of localhistory. \" Behind the specific issues at stakefor historians of science and religion loom very important questions that cut to the core of contemporary historical inquiry. Does complexity, with its insistence on the localandtheparticular, necessarily run counterto efforts to synthesize and lookforpatterns? Can historiansfunction without master historical narratives, even though they necessarily blur contextual distinctives? In the followingforum, three prominent historians of science and religion consider these questions. Thisforum was supported by agrantfrom

The Complexity Thesis

The complexity thesis was originally laid out by John Brooke in his 1991 publication, *Science and Religion: Some Historical Perspectives.*

Essentially, Brooke argues that the ideas of science and religion constantly exist in a state of war.[150] The complexity thesis adopts a historical methodology that says the other models are too narrow of generalizations, and that one cannot simply define the relationship between science and religion, rather one must evaluate each specific historical circumstance through empirical analysis.

The Conflict Thesis

The conflict thesis originated from the above mentioned well-known publication of William Draper who first described the potential conflict between religion and faith on one side and science by empirical observation on the other side. [151]

"The laws of nature are written by the hand of God in the language of mathematics" from Galileo.

---

theJohn Templeton Foundation. Science, Religion, and Historical Complexity John Hedley Brooke Few discourses have been as riven with prejudice and polemical intentions as those concerning the mutual bearings of science and religion. The spectacular example of Richard Dawkins's anti-religious mission in The GodDelusion and the scathing reviews it has provoked in both the Fondón and New York Review of Books testify to ongoing battles and high public interest.' In the popular mind, science and religion are still engaged in a centuries-long war. Yet historians, drawing on longer perspectives and a rich diversity of interpretation, have contested the popular claim that science and religion are—and always have been—inevitably in conflict. Some of these historians, motivated by religious sympathies to \"set the record straight,\" have perhaps gone too far in the other direction. In contrast to the conflict thesis, a metanarrative of peace (or at least the potential for peace

150 Brooke.AS THE DISHNGUISHED HISTORIAN OF scienceJohn Hedley Brooke notes, that in a time when historians are deeply suspicious of metanarratives, there has been a decidedemphasis on historicalcomplexity. Nowhere is this more evidentthan in the history of science andreligion, a subjectto which Brooke has made substantial contributions. Inplace of the warfare metaphor, historians of science andreligion have adoptedan anti-essentialist approach, dubbedthe \"complexity thesis\" and often associated with Brooke's work. Close examination ofparticular historicalcontexts does not reveal \"some timeless inherent relationship\" between science and religion. But, as Brooke and Geoffrey Cantor warned in their Gifford Fectures, preoccupation withparticular contexts might dissolve \"thegreat issues that have been debated under the banner of 'science and religion' into thefragments of localhistory. \" Behind the specific issues at stakefor historians of science and religion loom very important questions that cut to the core of contemporary historical inquiry. Does complexity, with its insistence on the localandtheparticular, necessarily run counterto efforts to synthesize and lookforpatterns? Can historiansfunction without master historical narratives, even though they necessarily blur contextual distinctives? In the followingforum, three prominent historians of science and religion consider these questions. Thisforum was supported by agrantfrom theJohn Templeton Foundation. Science, Religion, and Historical Complexity John Hedley Brooke Few discourses have been as riven with prejudice and polemical intentions as those concerning the mutual bearings of science and religion. The spectacular example of Richard Dawkins's anti-religious mission in The GodDelusion and the scathing reviews it has provoked in both the Fondón and New York Review of Books testify to ongoing battles and high public interest.' In the popular mind, science and religion are still engaged in a centuries-long war. Yet historians, drawing on longer perspectives and a rich diversity of interpretation, have contested the popular claim that science and religion are—and always have been—inevitably in conflict. Some of these historians, motivated by religious sympathies to \"set the record straight,\" have perhaps gone too far in the other direction. In contrast to the conflict thesis, a metanarrative of peace (or at least the potential for peace

151 FLEMING, *John William Draper and the Religion of Science.*

"Science flies you to the moon, religion flies you into buildings"- from the atheist Victor Stenger, referencing the 9/11 attacks.[152]

The idea of the conflict thesis is that there will always be a conflict between science and religion.

For whatever the reasoning might be, whether it is moral versus immoral, reason versus ignorance, religious faith versus scientific proof, among many other conflicts, there is a preeminent divergence. This divergence between the two will always arise and will inevitably end in feuding. This issue is seen repeatedly in history and literature, science and reason on one side fighting religion and ignorance on the other, and vice versa.

The Independence Model

"Science investigates; religion interprets. Science gives man knowledge, which is power; religion gives man wisdom, which is control. Science deals mainly with facts; religion deals mainly with values. The two are not rivals." from Martin Luther King Jr.[153]

In the time leading up to the First World War, the strong sense of nationalism led to the development of an egocentric belief that some individuals or people or races were favored uniquely by divine providence.

Theologians and ministers of the time, wanting to fulfill their patriotic duty, assured the people that God was on their side. When the war was over, and the mass devastation it caused was so apparent, it did not seem like God was on anybody's side. This fueled the teachings of the Protestant most famous theologian of the 20th century, the Swiss Calvinist Karl Barth (1886-1968), who insisted that God was radically distinct (fully transcendent) from the world.[154] Science was a means to study a world that God is radically distinct from. Barth taught that there was only one exception to this core belief, Jesus Christ. He stood as the single point of when God and the world met. This model often appeals to existentialists, who believe that everything relates via the subjective and objective – with Theology pertaining to the former, and science the latter. Essentially, the main idea is

---

152   USERID43, "Victor Stenger, 1935 – 2014 - Freedom From Religion Foundation."
153   Rowell, *Making Sense of the Sacred.*
154   Nimmo, *The Oxford Handbook of Karl Barth.*

that both science and religion are completely independent of one other. If a conflict does arise, it is assumed that one or both sides are overstepping their boundaries.

However, then who sets the boundaries and acts as the authority? The answer to this question usually boils down to one's own personal faith.

The Dialogue Model

"The idea is not so much for science to change theology, or for theology to change science, but rather to see what each, considered on its own terms, might have to say about questions which arise because of the other."-from Daniel Halverson

Theorists that support the dialogue model believe that each enterprise such as science as well as religion has something of a distinct value to say to the other. Each has elements in common, yet others that keep them distinct. A prime example is comparing religions from pre-modernity, looking at their regions, and seeing how each shaped their regions definition of "science."

Europeans, through Christianity, believed that nature was intelligible, and therefore understandable. The thought that humans were made in the image of God led them believe that man's abilities for higher thought made them mostly God-alike (Thomas Aquinas's *adaequatio ad rem*). Hence people in this model would argue that the conversations between religion and science led to the overwhelming number of scientific discoveries in 15th century Europe, compared to other wealthier more stable civilizations of the time.

The Synthesis Model

The synthesis model is the one favored by Ian Barbour.[155] The main goal is to arrive at a unified worldview that incorporates the most essential ideas and insights from both science and theology. Barbour identified three main principles of reasoning within this model: natural theology, theology of nature, and process theology. Natural theology is based on reasoning about God through scientific evidence.

---

155   Barbour, *Religion and Science*."ISBN":"978-0-06-060938-2","language":"English","number-of-pages":"3
84","publisher":"HarperOne","publisher-place":"San Francisco","source":"Amazon","title":"Religion and
Science","author":[{"family":"Barbour","given":"Ian G."}],"issued":{"date-parts":[["1997",8,2]]}}],"schema":"https://
github.com/citation-style-language/schema/raw/master/csl-citation.json"}

Theology of nature is striving to understand God in a scientific context. One favoring this model would claim "*the appearance of randomness in nature is genuine, but that does not mean that God is not in overall.*"

The third, process theology, is the idea that God is continuously and harmoniously evolving with the universe. It is said that this principle is heavily influenced by the ideas of Plato.

Chapter Thirty-One

The Catholic Church and Its Relationship to Science

Historically, the Catholic Church in general has not had a honorable past accepting science as a part of reasoning development of the universe and creation in general. The inquisition was part of the dark ages for the Church, declaring whatever appeared to potentially oppose the Church's teachings or questioned theological dogmas as heresy and therefore, condemned the ideas and penalized or even killed the scientists. The issues arose when Scripture was read literally rather than as poetry or allegorical, meaning that human creation was seen for example that Eve was created from Adam's site and thus, not accepting theories of evolution.

One of modern concerns is that whatever man can find on internet searches and teaching materials from representatives of the Catholic Church regarding how much the Church supports and has supported science and scientific advances seems lacking the acceptance of mistakes made by church officials including former Popes throughout history. Undoubtedly, the Catholic Church is an active proponent of scientific research as evidenced by the fact that the first universities in Europe (meaning in the world) have been founded by the Church, and also by the fact that the Church hosts several research communities and institutions.

The *Pontifical Academy of Sciences* and the *Vatican Observatory* are examples of high level research institutions and communities with scientists of the highest international reputation as their members. Moreover, at the current time, the Vatican regularly organizes scientific conferences and meetings, either virtually or in person on basically all aspects for modern science through the *Pontifical Academy of Science* or the *Pontifical Academy for Life*. The Pontifical Academy of Sciences was established in 1936 by Pope Pius XI. The academy is under direct supervisor of the Pope, and its aim is to promote the progress of mathematical, physical and natural sciences, and the study of epistemological problems related thereto. Its members consist of well-established researchers including several Nobel prize winners. Membership cannot be applied for but is only as per recommendation from an existing member. Pope Benedict became a member of the academy as Joseph Kardinal Ratzinger based on his academic achievements as a theologian, he was appointed by Pope John Paul II.

As examples, there is a conference entitled "Ethics Education and New Technologies: Cooperation or Conflict", held June 23-25, 2022, at the Vatican; in September 2021, there was a workshop on "Public Health on Global Perspective, Pandemic, Bioethics, Future"; on July 1, 2021, there was an "International Roundtable on Vaccination"; in February 2020 there were the "Proceedings of the "Good" Algorithm? Artificial Intelligence: Ethics, Law, Health"; in September 2020, the "International Conference AI (Artificial Intelligence), Food for all, Dialoque and Experiences" was conducted, among many other scientific conferences. As such, the Catholic Church has not only accepted Darwin's theory of evolution, but in its attempt to modernize, is supporting all natural sciences without seeing those as a threat to faith or the Churches' teachings.

The discrepancy between the natural sciences and theology is wider as evidenced by the fact that modernism promotes sciences whereas faith might be neglected by many, which appears to be a progressive trend. The churches, in particular the Catholic Church, is losing followers, for several reasons.[156]

---

156 "The Catholic Church Is Losing Its Most Devoted Followers | HuffPost Null."

One reason is its former reluctance to accept scientific evidence for evolution as well its problem to keep younger and more liberal generations engaged. Another current reason why the Catholic Church loses even its most devoted followers is because of sexual abuse scandals conducted by Catholic priests all over the world, which creates animosity against strict traditional church rules while representing hypocrisy for decades by failing to adequately address raised concerns and following leads or abuse complaints.[157] At the current time it is up to the Vatican to appropriately address the current situation and make adequate adjustments and perform excommunications of those guilty of molestation besides the initiation of criminal investigations by the appropriate legal authorities.

In contrast to natural sciences such as mathematics, biology, physics, and astronomy, theology is not based on evidential knowledge but purely on divine revelation. By thus, the science of theology deals with God and the understanding of the natural world but is not revealed by natural demonstration, not like an experiment in biochemistry that uses enzymes to catalyze a distinct reaction or not like in in physics class while showing Newton's decomposition of sunlight using a prism.

Furthermore, theology is not to comprehended by philosophical argumentation - but in contrast by reason of credibility - based on personal faith, history, sacred Scriptures, and sacred tradition. In contrast, theology is somewhat contrary to philosophy, however, a relation between theology and philosophy is implied in the First Vatican Council of 1870, in *Dei Filius de Fide Catholica.*

Faith (in theology) and reason (in philosophy) is somewhat based on the Church's understanding of grace and nature, and according to the Catholic Church, theology requires philosophy as a necessary infrastructure.[158] Theology has the faith in God at its core, and this faith is above all sciences. As a natural result, faith should therefore never be compromised by natural occurrences, but stand way above those. What gives man consciousness, the

---

157   "Catholics Are Losing Faith in Clergy and Church after Sexual Abuse Scandal, Gallup Survey Says | CNN."
158   OP, *The Shape of Catholic Theology.*

freedom to make decisions to help others or to decide upon morals and ethical understanding, is God-given. The pre-requisite for any faith in Christianity is the existence of God as the creator and the reason behind everything, the mover who cannot be moved, according to St Thomas Aquinus.[159] Faith in God does not negate any scientific findings and thus, science is not a subject limited purely to atheists.

---

159   Aquinas, *The Summa Theologica of St. Thomas Aquinas.*

Chapter Thirty-Two

Thoughts on the Conflict Between Faith and Science on Immortality

In the following paragraphs, we evaluate the writings of different individuals including researchers and theologians on their view on immortality, and we will focus on the ongoing conflict between the natural sciences and religion or religious beliefs, in order to show that science does not invalidate faith, and that faith does not dispute sciences.

Before diving into the discussion, we will briefly objectify what science is. Science is not the all-or-nothing answer to all questions for humankind. Science in its purest definition describes a learned method that systematically evaluates natural findings by means of reproducible experiments. In that sense, the objective of science is to explain natural occurring phenomena in its context. Science therefore, is considered objective, and not sensitive to alterations based on the researcher performing the experiment or on the observer viewing and interpreting the results.

On the other hand, science can only prove (or disprove) whatever question is asked within the frame of a controlled condition, meaning under the circumstances evaluated and within the objects tested in a particular scenario under reproducible conditions. An example could be to test whether a specific newly developed medication (called drug A) is capable to reduce the size of a heart attack. The working hypothesis would then be that drug A *is able* to reduce the amount of necrosis (cell death) after a heart attack and by thus, reduces the area and the measured size of infarcted tissue in the heart. To test this hypothesis, we just need to answer the following question: Is drug A able to reduce heart attacks? The answer then has to be simply and precisely just: *yes* or *no.*

We then might design an experimental animal model in which a heart attack is created by suturing a coronary artery in a rodent model after thoracotomy in two groups of animals, those who receive drug A prior to the induction of the heart attack, and those who receive a placebo at a similar time in a similar fashion. After 4 weeks, the hearts are excised and the infarcted area within the left heart chambers are measured planimetrically to quantify the amount of infarcted tissue.

If the group receiving drug A shows statistically significant smaller infarcts compared to the placebo group, then we can claim that drug A reduced infarct size in this model, so the answer to our working hypothesis question: does drug A reduces heart attacks? will be: yes.

If however, we want to extrapolate these data to a different species or a different scenario, then we cannot make the assumption that drug A reduces heart attacks if given in a different manner. If the drug is administered after the coronary suture is paced (in contrast to our original design in which the drug was administered before the coronary occlusion), we have a completely different experimental design. If we change the species to mice rather than rats, we have a different experiment. If we excise the heart after 3 months rather than after 4 weeks, we also have created a different experimental model, or if we add another drug B before the coronary occlusion or if we give drug A not once but for 6 days in a row, then all of these protocols are at least somewhat different from our original experimental design and therefore, represent different experimental scenarios.

In other words, the scientific experiment only proves or disproves a working hypothesis within the specifics of a particular experimental setup

- but not beyond. Drug A reduced infarct sizes only in the experimental setting described in the methods of the current study protocol, but that does not mean drug A would do the same in case we would change any of the parameters in any possible way.

This is the point where the lay person oftentimes misreads experimental scientific data and generalizes specific study findings as being valid, even in other scenarios or even in humans, which is oftentimes far from the truth and might not be the case. Unfortunately, many scientific study results are used in such a misleading and untrue way by the guys on the next bar-stools who hardly know anything about the science or scientific methods but know very well how to talk and sell their ideas. Sounds harsh, but often-times is true.

In order to understand the conflict between faith and scientific findings, or simply, between religion and sciences, we will evaluate the writings of scholars in philosophy, biology and theology on the subject.

The Swiss Catholic theologian Hans Kueng (1928-2021) in his clas-sical work "Eternal Life?" from 1982 goes back to the origin of science, which all started with medicine.[160] The French revolutionary Marie-Jean Antoine-Nicolas de Caritat, Marquis de Condorcet (1743-1794) pro-claimed in his *Historical Presentation of the Human Mind* in 1794 the ultimate goal of medicine the abolition or postponement of death.[161] The *materialism controversy* was brough up in 1854 at a conference in Goettin-gen/Germany, which favored a new strictly empirical scientific approach that basically abandoned all philosophical or theological reservations and made religion nothing else than a private matter, and it even declared all scientists and physicians as atheists.

Moreover, the revolutionary dogma was that the belief in the human being, in science, completely replaced the belief in God (Kueng).[162]

The age of the Scientific Revolution started approximately in the 16th century, possibly with the Polish astronomer Nicolaus Copernicus' (1473-

---

160   ThriftBooks, "Eternal Life?"
161   "Marquis de Condorcet | Biography, Writings, & Facts | Britannica."
162   ThriftBooks, "Eternal Life?"

1543) publication on the revolutions of the heavenly spheres (*De Revolutionibus Orbium Coelestium*), which means that the center of the earth is not the center of the universe but rather a place near the sun. Copernicus' theories were denunciated by Tolosani and the Catholic Church (Westman: On the truth of Sacred Scripture).[163]

The Italian astronomer and physicist Galileo Galilei (1564-1642) has then been named the father of modern science and the scientific method, especially since he stated that "*the universe was written in the language of mathematics*" and supported the Copernican heliocentrism (the earth rotating around the sun), which offended the view of the Catholic Church and thus, resulted in an investigation by the Roman Inquisition in 1615, which concluded that these concepts were heretical. Galileo subsequently was forced to recant and was put under house arrest because of suspicion of heresy.

The scientific revolution then was completed with Isaac Newtons (1642-1727) *Principia* in 1687, which described the laws of motion and gravitation.

In addition to the predominance of science over religion, philosophers such as the German Ludwig Feuerbach (1804-1872) put the nail on the coffin of Christian beliefs in his publication *The Essence of Christianity* in 1841, arguing that God was a human invention and that religion is just a form of human self-consciousness, representing atheism.

At the end of the 19th century, the German philosopher Friedrich Nietzsche (1844-1900) declared that it was impossible for a human being to believe in God, and even declared Christianity a "*contradiction of life*". Shortly thereafter, the English biologist Charles Darwin (1809-1882) proposed his evolutionary theory, stating that all species have descended from common ancestors in an evolutionary process of adaptation with subsequent survival of the fittest traits by natural selection ("On the origin of species", 1859).[164]

Even though the Catholic Church initially unofficially dismissed the ideas of Darwin's evolution as opposing the writings in Sacred Scriptures,

---

163   Westman, *The Copernican Question*.
164   Darwin, *The Origin of Species*.'On the Origin of Species by Means of Natural Selection, or the Preservation of Favoured Races in the Struggle for Life';

the encyclical *Humani Generis* in 1950 under Pope Pius XII (1876-1958) confirmed that there is no intrinsic conflict between Christian beliefs and the widely accepted scientific theory of evolution, provided that Christians believe that God created all things, and therefore 'theistic evolution' is known as *evolutionary creation*.[165] Biblical text, in particular with regard to Genesis, therefore is read as allegorical rather than as literal.

Coming back to one of the greatest 20th century Catholic theologians, Karl Rahner stated that nature represents itself in the human being in that it consciously realizes its own existence for the first time (in contrast to all other species). Rahner also implied that the evolutionary process was directed toward the humans, according to Oliver Putz.[166] According to Rahner and his strict adherence to Catholic dogmatism, biologic evolution is the result of divine creation, combined with active self-transcendence, with one origin, self-realization, and one destination, as a unity of matter and spirit in the human being (*"beseelter Leib und leibhaftiger Geist"*).[167,168]

In this sense, science does not address the spirit since the materialistic approach of the natural sciences lacks any connection to or acceptance of the supernatural. In man, the material universe has become so that it can for the first time experience itself (*the absolute being*), and therefore, the infinite mystery of God, according to Rahner. His concept of nature-directed and God-created active self-transcendence as the underlying metaphysical principle of the evolutionary process is an approach to mediate a dialogue between Catholic theology and evolutionary biology.

Evolutionary diversity, therefore, is an aspect of God's self-communication.

The German philosopher and anthropologist Ludwig Feuerbach (1804-1872), who initially was a theologian but then criticized Christianity and became anti-religion, argued against a selfish belief in immortality.[169] Moreover, he postulated that God was not the creator, but man created God in his image and his imagination, *Homo homini Deus,* and the belief in immortality of man is the belief in the divinity of man.

---

165 "Humani Generis (August 12, 1950) | PIUS XII."
166 Putz, "Evolutionary Biology in the Theology of Karl Rahner."
167 McDermott, "The Christologies of Karl Rahner - II."
168 Putz, "Evolutionary Biology in the Theology of Karl Rahner."
169 "Feuerbach - Thoughts on Death and Immortality."

Darwin's Theory of Evolution versus Intelligent Design

The Catholic church came a long way in 1997, when Pope John Paul II (1920-2005) called the evolutionary theory for the first time *"more than a hypothesis"*. The Pope indirectly accepted the biological concept of evolution as a scientific fact which should not be contradicting the Churches dogmatic teachings.[170]

Moreover, Pope Benedict XVI (aka Joseph Kardinal Ratzinger, born 1927) even led a debate on evolution and he stated that the conflict between evolution and creationism was an *"absurdity"*, since evolution can as well coexist with faith, in particular since evolution is proven by sciences, appears to be now well accepted also by the church, and evolution and God's role in the creation do not exclude each other (MSNBC News, July 25, 2007).[171]

However, it should be mentioned in this context that the highly praised evolutionary theory is now heavily criticized by many, and even Darwin himself admitted that there are unexplainable facts to consider which might abolish the whole theory deep to its fundamental ideas[172]. Darwin argued that the evolution of living things occurred as a result of natural selection based on simple cellular entities towards multicellular organisms, which then became highly specialized until humans developed as a progress evolving from this concept. He defined evolution as organisms evolving through time with traits that enable them to adapt to their ever changing environment for survival and healthy offspring production. In natural selection the most fit ones and the ones who are able to adapt with the most heritable traits repopulate and further develop into more highly specialized and sophisticated organisms.

However, this widely accepted concept is now shaken by the findings of the Cambrian explosion, which resembles the emerge of many of the major phyla based on findings of fossils of thousands of highly specialized forms of life and animals that lived approximately 550 million years ago.

Even Darwin was aware of this fact and unable to explain, and evolutionary biologists argued since almost two centuries until this day that the

---

170   Facebook et al., "Evolution Is More Than a Theory, Pope Tells Scientists."
171   "Pope."
172   Darwin, *The Origin of Species*.'On the Origin of Species by Means of Natural Selection, or the Preservation of Favoured Races in the Struggle for Life';

precursors of the Cambrian explosion have just not been found, yet. Fact is, however, that obviously there might be no precursors as Darwin expected, which means that evolution is unable to explain the co-existence of thousands of different forms of life at an early stage of life development.

Today, many leading scientists are now rejecting Darwin's theory of evolution because the Cambrian explosion showed that highly specialized animals just appeared in the Fossil records without any evidence of any fossils representing prior ancestors before them. These findings present compelling evidence for an all powerful *designing intelligence* in the history of creation of life.

The scientist and author Stephen Meyers called it the *Mystery of the Missing Fossils* in his popular New York Times bestseller book "Darwin's Doubt", since the precambrian strata in the earth's layers find no evidence of any simpler forms of prior generations of animals[173]. Furthermore, Meyers asks how a process according to NeoDarwinism could be able to build complex forms of life abruptly during a relatively narrow window of geologic time. Since all life is dependent on information in DNA as genetic codes, evolution does not explain the formation of DNA from simple to complex, since even the simplest DNA is a complex structure in itself. The naïve idea that hundreds of millions of years ago some atoms and molecules accidently came together by chance and then miraculously developed into a structure that suddenly became a cell and had vital functions unscientific, more likely is that all the development is dependent on an intelligent design, which supports the idea of a higher power or God as the creator off everything[174].

Arguments For And Against Irreducible Complexity

In addition to the above, the biologist Michael Behe introduced the concept of the *irreducible complexity*, which also supports and tries to confirm the idea of intelligent design.[175] In simple words, what Behe argues is that in order to maintain the function of certain complex systems, it is required that the individual components are in place. It is impossible to reduce the complexity of the complex systems by removing any components, since any

---

173   Meyer, *Darwin's Doubt*.
174   *Return of the God Hypothesis*.
175   Behe, *A Mousetrap for Darwin*.

material reduction would automatically delete its entire functionality, as evidenced by his famous *mouse trap model*.

The mousetrap contains five different independent parts which provide the materials and the mechanisms that enables it to catch a mouse: the wooden platform, a spring, a holding bar, the hammer and a catch. Every single one of these individual parts are necessary to make the mouse trap work. If one part is missing, the trap is useless. For instance, if you remove the catch, you cannot set up the trap and it will not catch a mouse. Even removal of the holding bar will not trap a mouse, too. Therefore, only the design of the trap in its entirety with all of its parts in the correct place and connected to each other will make the parts a functional unity with the ability to catch a mouse.

Thinking this concept through makes it very unlikely to imagine that there could be an incidental way that a random selection of wooden and metal parts put blindly together could miraculously create a functional unity resembling a mouse trap spontaneously - without someone designing it from the beginning. Behe basically repeats Aristotle, who stated in *Metaphysics*, "The whole is more than the sum of its parts." [176]

Similarly, the complex nature and structure of DNA as the basic of life therefore likely cannot just randomly occur by chance - but does require intelligent design. The debate is still ongoing among scientists on the issues of Darwin's evolutionary theory on one hand and the possible existence of intelligent design on the other hand. Even more, whatever intelligent design represents naturally depends on the view of the proponents of either theory. Theologians will declare intelligent design as proof of God's creation, while some biologists might consider non-divine forces as being responsible for life as it developed, while others believe that the concept of intelligent design is not a scientifically proven finding (which I personally would oppose to).

Moreover, in the same context, Behe argues that our very complex immune system as a different example, cannot be simply explained as a result of spontaneous mutation and random selection to develop to its miraculous version what it became for human survival, he states that "*clonal selection,*

---

176   Aristotle, *The Metaphysics*.

antibody diversity, and the complement system - are irreducibly complex and pose massive challenges to a putative step-by-step evolution". [177]

Behe's scientific opponents, however, accuse him of either not evaluating or even not knowing the scientific literature sufficiently, which claims that antibody genes are capable of recombination to develop further in evolution, a process named the "transposon hypothesis." This hypothesis states that any transposon could have invaded the genome of any animal, possibly via any bacterial infection 450 million years ago, which then could have let to the splitting of a gene into segments. When cells then read the host genes, bacterial genes were read instead, leading to the cutting out of a transposon which then was placed into and changed the genome, which then could develop further. This hypothetical process was elegantly described in scientific details by Katherine Applegate in 2010. [178] Of interest, Applegate states further that some of Behe's critics are not just atheists supporting Darwinism, but even deeply committed Christians who see evidence that irreducibly complex structures and systems have developed gradually through natural, evolutionary processes, which does not automatically deny a divine order.

The debate between atheistic scientists and representatives of the Christian churches is still going on, as even recently evidenced by a widely viewed discussion between the evolutionary biologist and self-declared atheist Richard Dawkins (born 1941), who is well known for his stand against creationism ("*The God Delusion*"),[179] and the Archbishop of Canterbury Rowan Williams (Baron Williams of Oystermouth, born 1950) at Oxford University in 2012 on the origin of human life and the universe. As expected, the 90-minute debate that was broadcasted and is visible on Youtube, did neither reach any conclusions nor any rapprochement between the atheist scientist with his views on the absolute unnecessity of a God in our modern lives on one side and the theologian and archbishop who leaves faith open to a personal decision on the other side.[180]

---

177   Behe, *Darwin's Black Box.*
178   "Behe and Irreducible Complexity."
179   Dawkins, *The God Delusion.*
180   University of Oxford, *Richard Dawkins versus Rowan Williams.*

Chapter Thirty-Three

Thoughts on Immortality for Health Care Providers

Health care providers such as physicians and nurses mostly are dealing with sickness and suffering of patients with incurable and progressive diseases and the processes of end-of-life care and dying - contrasting patient expectations, disbeliefs, disappointments, resentments until final acceptance of impending death. More recently, with the populistic announcements of scientific advances in modern medicine, anti-aging and immortality research, there are additional challenges health care providers are facing with regard to unrealistic treatment options or expectations for miraculous cures leading to much longer lives from the patients or more often from their family members or care givers.

Dealing with chronically sick patients with progressive diseases and dying patients on one site while accepting and supporting biotechnologic advances in modern science on the other site can be thought-provoking, even more for those who share Christian beliefs in the resurrection and everlasting life.

Providing maximal therapy based on availability of technologic options and appropriate provider expertise is recommended based on the circumstances and prognosis. In case of futility, however, shared decision making should be attempted between the provider and the patient and/or his/her caregivers regarding the options of palliative therapy, comfort care measures or hospice care for symptom relief and improvement of quality of life in cases of incurable diseases that likely will result in death in the very near future.

Independent on the personal beliefs and religious faith of physicians or nurses, any discussions about an afterlife or even immortality are beyond what health care providers usually stipulate in this situation but adhere to their professional duties in medicine while these other discussions are reserved to non-medical care givers, family members, clergy or spiritual advisors, if requested by the patient. In other words, the medical professional has a duty to primarily provide medical care (rather than spiritual care), even though passion and empathy as well as psychological support should be an essential supplemental part of standard medical care.

On the other hand, spiritual care can be offered by physicians as part of a holistic approach to care, as proposed by Pembroke (a theologian).[181] A recent survey among physicians demonstrated that medical doctors hold divided perceptions of the psychological impact of patients' religious beliefs and practices at the end of life. Many see prayers as having positive psychological impacts for patients. The authors even suggested a formal training in spiritual care to improve patient communication with regard to their religion and spirituality.[182] Our group recently demonstrated the beneficial effects of faith (independent on religion) and prayers among hospitalized patients with chronic heart failure.[183]

Moreover, a questionnaire among 177 adult patients revealed that fifty-one percent described themselves as religious, and 90% believed that prayers may influence recovery from an illness. Many but not all patients

181 Pembroke, "Appropriate Spiritual Care by Physicians."
182 Thompson et al., "Physicians' Religious Characteristics and Their Perceptions of the Psychological Impact of Patient Prayer and Beliefs at the End of Life.""plainCitation":"Thompson et al., "Physicians' Religious Characteristics and Their Perceptions of the Psychological Impact of Patient Prayer and Beliefs at the End of Life.""","noteIndex":177},"citationItems":[{"id":389,"uris":["http://zotero.org/users/8373236/items/DYMGGCDM"],"uri":["http://zotero.org/users/8373236/items/DYMGGCDM"],"itemData":{"id":389,"type":"article-journal","abstract":"BACKGROUND:: Physicians who are more religious or spiritual may report more positive perceptions regarding the link between religious beliefs/practices and patients' psychological well-being.\nMETHODS:: We conducted a secondary data analysis of a 2010 national survey of US physicians from various specialties (n = 1156
183 Naghi et al., "The Effects of Spirituality and Religion on Outcomes in Patients with Chronic Heart Failure."

welcomed a physician-directed inquiry about their spiritual or religious beliefs in the event that they become seriously ill in this particular cohort.[184]

There are now efforts in place to foster spiritual education for medical students as evidenced by a project called "*The Sacred Sites of Houston*" in 2021 that resulted in increased awareness among the trainees of the importance of religion and spirituality in patient-provider relationships, especially at end of life care situations.[185]

A recently published analysis by Lopez-Tarida et al. in 2021 revealed that barriers for physicians to address spiritual care for their patients are lack of appropriate guidance and training, lack of time, as well as unfamiliarity and fear addressing spiritual dimensions in the frame of medical management.[186]

While on one hand the medical providers' personal religious beliefs should neither influence any medical decisions for or against any treatment nor affect any medical information provided to a patient about outcome or prognosis, on the other hand an evaluation of the patients' faith and beliefs and expectations should be conducted in order to support shared decision-making about therapies, especially for end-of life care, palliative care for chronic progressive incurable diseases, and also in critically ill children.[187]

Even though there should be a clear distinction between practical medicine and practiced religion, as a holistic management of any sick individual, the patient's physical, mental, psychological and spiritual condition needs to be taken into consideration as a whole unit of a human being and thus, appropriately addressed in order to support compliance, treatment

---

184   Ehman et al., "Do Patients Want Physicians to Inquire about Their Spiritual or Religious Beliefs If They Become Gravely Ill?"

185   King et al., "The Sacred Sites of Houston."

186   López-Tarrida, de Diego-Cordero, and Lima-Rodríguez, "Spirituality in a Doctor's Practice.""plainCitation":"López-Tarrida, de Diego-Cordero, and Lima-Rodríguez, "Spirituality in a Doctor's Practice."","noteIndex":181},"citationItems":[{"id":395,"uris":["http://zotero.org/users/8373236/items/5KWLBJM3"],"uri":["http://zotero.org/users/8373236/items/5KWLBJM3"],"itemData":{"id":395,"type":"article-journal","abstract":"INTRODUCTION: It is becoming increasingly important to address the spiritual dimension in the integral care of the people in order to adequately assist them in the processes of their illness and healing. Considering the spiritual dimension has an ethical basis because it attends to the values and spiritual needs of the person in clinical decision-making, as well as helping them cope with their illness. Doctors, although sensitive to this fact, approach spiritual care in clinical practice with little rigour due to certain facts, factors, and boundaries that are assessed in this review.\ nOBJECTIVE: To find out how doctors approach the spiritual dimension, describing its characteristics, the factors that influence it, and the limitations they encounter.\nMETHODOLOGY: We conducted a review of the scientific literature to date in the PubMed, Scopus, and CINAHL databases of randomised and non-randomised controlled trials, observational studies, and qualitative studies written in Spanish, English, and Portuguese on the spiritual approach adopted by doctors in clinical practice. This review consisted of several phases: (i

187   Uveges et al., "The Influence of Parents' Religiosity or Spirituality on Decision Making for Their Critically Ill Child."

adherence, cooperation and an open communication for a successful and satisfying physician-patient relationship. This includes oftentimes repeated education provided by the health care provider to the patients and their care givers and family members about the disease and possible treatment options as well as an honest interpretation on expected outcomes rather than exaggerated visions of futuristic therapies that might or might not lead to biologic immortality a later time.

For the health care providers it also requires the self-explanatory re-emphasis and acceptance of the fact that no human ever in history became immortal in this world (so far) - but died, also for the sake of the psychological wellbeing of the health care providers in case of a breakdown caused by devastation as a result of failed therapies.

In a philosophical sense, we need to be reminded what the ultimate goal of medicine is: according to common understanding it is the relief of pain and suffering, alleviation of symptoms, prevention of harm, restoration of function, and prolongation of life whenever possible, the promotion of health and the prevention of disease, and promotion of a peaceful death, and the cure of disease when possible and the care of those who cannot be cured.[188] As such the practicing physician should not be just specific organ-oriented but needs to address all aspects of health including but not limited to bodily organ function, psychological issues, anxiety and fear, psychosocial aspects and spiritual characteristics, as long as it supports the quality of care for a patient. Besides the challenges such an approach consumes for health care providers, lack of time, reduction of reimbursements, and political and economic issues such as managed care provisions to cut costs provide additional tribulations in today's health care system.[189]

---

188   Callahan, "Managed Care and the Goals of Medicine."
189   Callahan.

Chapter Thirty-Four

Thoughts on Death and the Afterlife

D ealing with dying patients is a challenge for health care providers, which is quite different from experiences individuals underwent when they were going to die - but survived. The comprehensions of dying people, as published by researchers but also by lay people - though of interest to learn about the visions of light and peace and oftentimes a view from above the dying body by the individual himself - does not really contribute much to the concept of immortality or the path someone goes through from life to death or to a life outside our understanding.

According to Hans Kueng, these experiences are those of dying, rather than of death, which is the final destination of dying (but those who reported their experiences actually did not go to the final destination of death, at least not at that time).[190] Moreover, these experiences do not give any insight into a possible life after death, even though postulated as such by those who envisioned the stage of dying in one version or another.

---

190   ThriftBooks, "Eternal Life?"

The thought of an afterlife sooner or later affects every single individual on earth. At the current time, there is even more fear than hope, in particular in view of possibilities we have not dreamt of a few years ago, such as the devastation of the earth through climate change, pandemics such as COVID-19, nuclear holocaust, economic collapse, alien invasion, a third world war (which appears closer than ever in our lifetime right now) or – as demonstrated in a recently released movie entitled *"Don't look up"* (2021), the possibility of a meterorite collision with a disastrous outcome to eliminate all life on earth or earth in its totality, which resembles the movie *"Melancholia"* from 2011.

One might even wonder why the richest people in the world (again), fly into space (such as Jeff Bezos or Elon Musk in 2021) or as the character in the movie who fled the collision by space flight escape. Matthew Wolf-Meyer describes the possibilities of an apocalyptic anthropology in his book *"Theory of the World to Come"*, which still "needs to instill curiosity".[191] That curiosity is what makes us want to learn and to study, but also which supports the human's belief in something else to follow after our earthly existence.

The world as it is will end, at one time, even though the predictions of futurologists are way beyond our life spans. Science can bring humanity only that far, but it cannot and never will be able to predict the future of the world or what will follow, after we die. In view of this understanding, faith is not only an antique belief, but also a motivation, a strength, a mystic, a tradition, a communion, a community, and a support to deal with the unknown beyond our comprehension and experiences.

Despite all advances in technology and ideas of decoding life mankind has still not completely accepted that there are things that cannot be explained by means of scientific deduction and analysis, such as our consciousness, why things happen, why people die, and if there is everlasting life beyond the sphere of our common understanding.

What is the alternative? Even the personal and philosophical attempts of intensification, extrapolation and mutation will usually result in either acceptance of our helplessness or resignation which then might lead to mate-

---

191   Wolf-Meyer, *Theory for the World to Come.*

rialize the world through more devastating inaction, a plausible theory postulated by Wolf-Meyer.[192] This kind of anthropologic speculation, however, lacks any innate willingness to consider a sense of higher power or God as a creator, mover and shaker, which then in turn diminishes the magnificence of human life to a natural incident rather than a created and conscious existence with a higher purpose or destination.

"*Unfortunately, the actual characteristic of this world is its past*" (Franz Kafka, 1883-1924).

While faith in religions and religious teachings dissipate to some degree in modern times, faith in natural sciences has peaked during the 20th and 21st century, especially as a result of wider and easier access to scientific data and news and its practical and life changing usability and utilization (such as the use of smart phones for everyone).

At the current time, however, we see a dissipation of faith in the sciences, which contradicts anyone's objective anticipation. Suddenly, man can become a pseudo-scientist and expert of all by reading social media as evidenced by all the "*COVID-19 experts*" that appeared on separate news channels since the beginning of 2020. Out of nowhere, every news outlet (even entertainment channel shows) now had a COVID-19 expert talking medicine, while in fact many of these – while looking good on camera and talking and sounding well – hardly ever have seen or treated a real COVID-19 patient. In addition, many so-called experts openly argue against vaccine efforts that clearly have shown to save lives worldwide. All these facts lead to a trend among several members of the broad public in not only losing faith in science[193] (and more, in politics) but even distrusting scientific facts, as described already in a historic perspective 40 years ago by Cohen.[194] This fact is even exaggerated in today's COVID-19 pandemic but is in strict contrast to critical substantiated reviews by scientific professionals. The rejection of critical study results that are often designed as randomized, double blind and even sometimes placebo-controlled as well as a low threshold for popular

---

192   {Citation}
193   Maddox, "The Prevalent Distrust of Science."
194   Cohen, "The Fear and Distrust of Science in Historical Perspective."

alternatives demonstrating an independent attitude and lack of any sense of indoctrination are all manifestations of this trend[195], which is particularly severe and can be dangerous if they result in avoidance of scientifically recommended measures (such as COVID-19 vaccinations).

This in turn can be disastrous, not only for the individual but also for the community, as seen within regions with low COVID-19 vaccination rates with raising hospital admissions and increased numbers of death cases worldwide.

The current public "war against science" resembles the known culture war between religion and science where science is increasingly associated with atheism[196], thus creating even more conflicts between those who have faith and those who believe in scientifically reproducible experimental data.

195   Guidotti, "Between Distrust of Science and Scientism."
196   Simpson and Rios, "Is Science for Atheists?"

Chapter Thirty-Five

Medicine for Immortality

From a natural scientific point of view, the ultimate medicine for immortality might be a combination of stem cell therapy and biogenetic manipulation, which is feasible and will be available in one form or another in the very near future. Realistically, however, this might not be not leading to biologic immortality, but rather to prolongation of life.

From a religious point of view, in particular from a Roman Catholic perspective, the (one and only) medicine for immortality, however, is - according to Ignatius of Antioch - since almost 2000 years, the Eucharist. Feeding from Christ's own Eucharistic flesh and blood is the "*medicine*" that is supposed to prepare us to pass through the process of dying and death to the glory of resurrection with everlasting life. The Holy Communion is the source and the energy of our true life in Christ. This was recently popularized by the current Pope Francis stating that the Eucharist is medicine for the "field hospital", which resembles the Church. Faith in this sense, becomes the vehicle for using the Eucharist as the ultimate medicine, the ultimate technology to create eternal life.

Religion, in particular Roman Catholicism, accepts life with death, but its faith is focused on the life after death by resurrection from the dead. Medicine on the other hand, focuses on avoiding death, if possible, or at least delaying it.

In order to better comprehend the facts that science and religion are not contrasting each other in this regard, one need to recapitulate in simple terms that the goal of medicine and science is to defy death. Christian belief and Church teachings, on the other hand, do neither abolish dying nor death at all. In contrast, according to Sacred Scripture Jesus proclaimed:

> *I am the resurrection and the life. Whoever believes in me, though he die, yet shall he live. (John 11:25, ESV)*

> *Or:*

> *Jesus said to her, I am the resurrection and the life, he that believeth in me, though he were dead, yet shall he live (John 11;25, KJV).*

> *Truly, truly, I say to you, whoever hears my word and believes him who sent me has eternal life. He does not come into judgement, but has passed from death to life. (John 5:24, ESV).*

In Christianity, therefore, death is not denied, it is part of life. Man dies but is resurrected after death. The resurrection is beyond what science can evaluate.

Chapter Thirty-Six

The Cryonic Movement

T he quest for immortality has created further ideas, concepts, and businesses. The cryonic movement as an example, does not really deal with immortality as a continuation of life at this or any defined time in the future. It is based on the fact is that cells can be frozen to be kept in a halted state for many years but then can be "revitalized" and are able to develop upon de-freezing. This concept is used since decades by freezing sperm cells and oocytes, for example for egg preservation, or even fertilized donor embryos for infertility treatments. These embryos are in a rested state deep frozen at -191 degrees Celsius and can be stored for decades. Upon thawing, these embryos can be implanted in the uterus and metabolic activity resumes, cells divide, and an entire human organism will then develop.

The so-called *"Cryonics"* use this concept to consider keeping their brain or bodies frozen immediately after death with the hope, that at one time - once biotechnology has advanced further - they can be thawed and restored to life, then benefitting from advances in modern medicine to keep them vital and healthy - a concept that has never been proven but has an increasing number of followers based on pure trust or *faith* (in a secularistic meaning) in that concept. Cryonics are considered *reductive materialists* and as such, secularists, seem to be challenging the predominant medical, legal, and scientific views of death, but possibly also any religious or philosophical meaning of life and death.[197] Cryonics are legally dead, but for their followers and their custodians at the cryopreservation company such as Alcor, they are not dead, but what they call *de-animated*.

The issues are manifold, but include the following:

1. There is no guarantee that anyone will be ever thawed.
2. There is no guarantee that after thawing, the body could be re-animated.
3. It is not sure even if the body or parts of it could be re-animated, if that body could survive for any given time afterwards.
4. Even if thawed and reanimated and alive, would the body not be in a similar state as prior to his/her death, i.e., old and frail and sick and full of degenerative diseases, heart failure or cancer?

Basically, the cryogenic movement appears almost similar to the idea leading to the mumification processes performed by ancient Egyptian pharaohs such as Tutankhamun during the 18 dynasty who reigned 1332 – 1323 BC, among others, to preserve their bodies for a world or an afterlife to come. In the mummies, however, all internal organs including the brain were removed and dried, and only the heart was re-placed into the embalmed body.

From a medical and scientific point of view, one of the main concerns is that even if the cryonic process might be able to conserve certain cell types like skin cells, hair cells among few others, it is unlikely that brain structure or heart structure can be appropriately preserved upon revivification. Without ongoing brain perfusion by a beating heart, brain cells start to die within a few minutes after cessation of circulation, and decay begins. Even if cryopreservation will be initiated within hours after death (what the companies promise), after a short delay (7 minutes) brain tissue and heart tissue is irreversible damaged so that even a preservation at that stage will not be able to keep the brain in a condition similar it status quo prior to death.

On the Alcor website, on the first page it is mentioned that *"cryonics is a scientific approach to extend human life that does not violate any religious*

---

197   Farman, *On Not Dying.*

beliefs or their principles". Cryonics, however, has never been shown to extend human life and its outcome is actually purely based on the secular faith of their followers in its concept rather than on any scientific data.

Cryonics is considered by its defenders as a precondition for future revivification.[198] At its current state, it does represnts a modern mumification process of the body based on a secular belief in a vague possibility of a future advance in a science that has not been defined, yet, but does neither prevent death, nor does it lead to immortality. For Christians, however, it does not matter whether a body is preserved in whatever form or is not preserved, since only the faith-based resurrection of body and soul after death is supposed to provide everlasting life.

---

198   Caire, "[Cryogenics]."

Chapter Thirty-Seven

Immortality from a Philosophical, Religious and Populistic Point of View

I mmortality in philosophy is usually defined as the indefinite continuation of the mental or spiritual existence of the human being in the form of its soul or even of body and soul. Immortality in a religious sense usually is seen either as a reward of a good life (conditional immortality) or the human destiny by divine nature to everlasting existence in another environment (heaven) or the physical and spiritual anastasis, (return back to life after death) of human beings.[199],[200]

Philosophical or religious immortality is the basis for faith, philosophical teachings, and doctrines of the churches but has never been experimentally reproduced or proven scientifically.

For clarification and to distinguish the philosophical/religious immortality we might call it "eternal existence".

Immortality in a biological sense is defined as the ongoing existence of metabolic activities, biochemical pathways and maintained integrity of

---

199   Ritchie, "Theories of Immortality."
200   "The Case for Conditional Immortality - J. W. Wenham."

cellular and tissue structure and function, either without undergoing senescence (cellular aging) or without necrosis or apoptosis (different forms of cell death).[201,202]

Natural immortality so far, has been only demonstrated in a certain jelly fish and worm species and is the current focus of biotechnology as part of medical, anti-aging, genetic, biochemistry, molecular biology and regenerative research as well as artificial intelligence.[203]

For clarification and to distinguish natural immortality (from biologic and other types of immortality, see above), one might call it *"everlasting existence"*.

The difference between eternal existence and everlasting existence is basically the difference between philosophical thinking and/or religious faith and biotechnological possibilities. Moreover, *eternal* immortality can be seen as time-independent (in divinity), while *everlasting* immortality is time-dependent (in humanity).

While medicine attempts to relief suffering from diseases, pain or other symptoms or loss of organ function or disability, different cultures, religions, and spiritual communities use faith in a higher power or in God to ease sufferings from physical or psychological pain. In this context, faith and religion with prayers and spiritual support on one site and medicine, technology and scientific research on the other site are not contradicting each other but should be complimentary in providing help to the individual human being and even in saving and prolongation of lives, though not everlasting or eternal, but for a worthwhile. In this context, the difference between religious and natural or biological immortality is just - *time*.

Is immortality biologically possible? Does biology and sciences replace religious faith? What is the physician's role in this context? We attempted to answer these questions in the present book:

Yes, some degree of biologic immortality or life prolongation will be in part possible in the near future;

---

201   Schwarz et al., "Myocyte Degeneration and Cell Death in Hibernating Human Myocardium."
202   Kunapuli, Rosanio, and Schwarz, ""How Do Cardiomyocytes Die?"
203   Walter, *Immortality, Inc.*

No, sciences do never replace faith in God and religion does not contradict sciences;

The physician should use his medical knowledge and address the patients' spirituality as part of a holistic care approach, in particular at end-of-life situations or for chronic (incurable) illnesses.

All unconscious cognitive processes such as thoughts, perceptions, memories, emotions, will and imaginations can be personified as the indivisible soul – or the *mind*.[204] The physical body is degenerating over time and is exposed to diseases such as cancer, infections, trauma, or other conditions leading to organ dysfunction. The soul however, usually is not supposed to be affected by physical injury and therefore, might continue to live indefinitely, at least in theory.

Our human body is mortal, and death of the body translates to death of the human individual, and this condition is considered irreversible, and death is final, at least in a biologic sense. If there is resurrection of body and soul (according to Christianity), meaning re-incarnation of the person after death, it is unexplainable whether the resurrected body/human then would be in his/her state similar to that prior to his/her earthly death - or in a different state.

Faith does not translate into a continuation of life in misery with fragility and sickness, which oftentimes might be the condition a priori just prior to death. In contrast, faith in resurrection of the body translates to eternal life of the individual in heaven (or Nirvana or somewhere else) in a state considered to be immune towards diseases, injuries, infections, degeneration or aging, which resembles a *"paradisian"* place beyond our imagination and beyond the opportunities of investigative research.

The common denominator between the different religions on the idea of immortality tends to be the spiritual or divine nature attributed to it, having in some cases the prolongation of life as a historical account within their pages that does not seem to be conceivable anymore, and therefore, barely depicted. The idea of eternity, a never-ending life, or an afterlife could

---

204   Pandya, "Understanding Brain, Mind and Soul."

be conjugated as a notion that we can call "*permanence.*" Depending on the religion, *permanence* could be achieved either by the spirit, soul, or body. The spiritual energy or soul could be comprehended as an "epitome" that works as an avatar for the conscious mind to achieve *permanence.*[205]

If the soul is immortal in a philosophical and religious context, the question remains whether or not biotechnology can be advanced to the extent to achieve immortality of the body. There is a major populistic interest in the quest for immortality, now more than ever, possibly due to the financial means and the availability of an abundance of resources such as laboratories, researchers, and well-equipped technology.[206]

Is the human race capable of reprograming cells to an embryonic stage where age is just a number, and continuous regeneration can be the possible answer to all ailments ever witnessed in life on this planet? Does interference with nature's destiny as we understand it today negate faith and religious beliefs? In other words, is it wrong to manipulate nature in which death can be seen not only as an accepted but even a welcoming destiny that might lead us to eternal life in heaven by attempting to prolong our earthly existence? Moreover, is humankind on the path to gain biotechnological methods to finally defy aging, diseases and death, which than might make faith in religion and in everlasting life obsolete?

There is a philosophical, religious but also intellectual challenge for physicians and healthcare providers dealing with guideline-oriented therapies while oftentimes facing patient requests for therapies beyond current possibilities of success but considered to represent futile measures.

To date, doctors are reacting to medicine either by treating symptoms and organ dysfunction after its occurrence. Nonetheless, present-day medical science is advancing to the ultimate goal of regeneration (using stem cell therapy, as an example) - versus reaction.

---

205   Pettus, "PERMANENCE."God, as enumerated by Mary Baker Eddy in \"Science and Health with Key to the Scriptures,\" a thoughtful student of Christian Science found great comfort in perceiving that the essence of every one of them was p...", "container-title":"The Christian Science Journal", "language":"en-US","title":"PERMANENCE","URL":"https:// journal.christianscience.com/shared/view/2eqvu4kjwys?s=f", "author":[{"family":"Pettus","given":"Maude"}], "accessed":{"da te-parts":[["2021",12,2]]}, "issued":{"date-parts":[["1937",12,1]]}}}, "schema":"https://github.com/citation-style-language/ schema/raw/master/csl-citation.json"}
206   Walter, *Immortality, Inc.*

As long as humankind has to deal with diseases (which likely will be as long as humankind in its present form exists), we should not forget the power of the mind in the processes of healing. We recently studied the effects of religious beliefs and prayers independent on religious denomination on hospitalized patients with heart failure, which demonstrated improved outcomes in believers compared to individuals who do not believe in anything and do not pray.[207]

In contrast to the past, more advances have been achieved than ever before in modern medicine and technology to understand the processes of aging and cellular death as well as the potential interference with what we call "*natural processes*". In other words, at the current time, many believe in the possibility of biologic immortality or at least prolongation of life by either manipulating age-related processes by genetic programming or by using regenerative medicine instead of reactive medicine to repair damage using stem cells and other methods.[208]

Technology has advanced incredibly in these fields so that prolongation of life is already a possibility today with further expectations in the not too far future. Whether or not natural immortality of the human race will be achievable at any time, however, remains questionable.

From a physician's point of view, we need to remind ourselves that advances in science and technology are often times not applicable for practical medicine, yet. In other words, patients with underlying progressive malignancies such as metastatic cancer or end stage heart failure for example, are still going to die, and as physicians we oftentimes remain unsuccessful in our efforts to defy death.

---

207   Naghi et al., "The Effects of Spirituality and Religion on Outcomes in Patients with Chronic Heart Failure."

208   Helmy et al., "Stem Cells and Regenerative Medicine." the promise of other stem cell populations for tissue replacement and repair remains unachieved. When considering cell-based interventions for personalized medicine, the factors influencing therapeutic success and safety are more complicated than for traditional small-molecule pharmacological agents and protein biologics. Failure to progress personalized stem cell therapies to the clinic has resulted from complications that include an incomplete understanding of developmental programs and the diversity of host-donor interactions. In order to more rapidly extend the use of stem cells to the clinic, a better understanding of the different stem cell sources and the implications of their host interactions is required. In this review, we introduce the currently available sources and highlight recent literature that instructs the potential and limitations of their use.","container-title":"Therapeutic Delivery","DOI":"10.4155/tde.10.57","ISSN":"2041-5990","issue":"5","journalAbbreviation":"Th er Deliv","language":"eng","note":"PMID: 21113422\nPMCID: PMC2990533","page":"693-705","source":"PubMed","title":"Stem cells and regenerative medicine: accomplishments to date and future promise","title-short":"Stem cells and regenerative medicine","volume":"1","author":[{"family":"Helmy","given":"Karim Y."},{"family":"Patel","given":"Shyam A."},{"family":"Silverio","given":"Kimberly"},{"family":"Pliner","given":"Lillian"},{"family":"Rameshwar","given":"Pranela"}],"issued":{"date-parts":[["2010",11]]}}]},"schema":"https://github.com/citation-style-language/schema/raw/master/csl-citation.json"}

In his most read book "Jesus von Nazareth" Joseph Ratzinger, then Pope Benedict XVI, stated: "*Ohne Sterben gibt es keine Gottesgemeinschaft und keine Erloesung*", meaning that without dying, there is no communion with God and no salvation.[209] One might argue that with immortality of the human being (without dying and without death), there is no God in human life, either existent, or even necessary.

The concept of the Martin Heidegger's (1889-1976) philosophy, which was essential for the thoughts and writings of the Catholic theologian Karl Rahner and others in the 20th century, is that we recognize the finite end of our life.[210] This existential reality that forms the philosophical concept of existentialism is what moves us, shapes us, and motivates us in our everyday being - but also in our hopes and dreams. Without the knowledge of the pending cessation of our earthly existence, most likely there would be no supernatural existential sense for our lives (Rahner), and that would make part of the supernatural, part of the belief and faith possibly superfluously.[211]

If we can achieve natural or at least biologic immortality by means of modern biotechnology and gene manipulation and create a human species that resembles hydras, jelly fishes or worms with unlimited regenerative capacities and lack of aging or mortality, why then would we even need faith in God, religion or any spirituality? Would not life then render faith obsolete?

If so, on the other hand, where would our consciousness be, our drive to be just and live a moral life, our fears and dreams, and our goals to achieve a legacy, whether it is for our immediate family or for the community? Would everlasting life also mean we do not need any salvation for our sins, would be there no grief since we never would lose anyone close to us, and we do not need to worry about punishment, diseases, frailty or sufferings at all? At this point we are – fortunately - far way from any of these possibilities.

A recent article by Ethan Siegel in Forbes Magazine was entitled with a negative answer (even though there was no question asked). The article received much attention since the title actually answered one of the most prominent questions for scientists but also for believers, entitled "*No, science

209   Ratzinger, *Jesus von Nazareth*.
210   "Being and Time (Harper Perennial Modern Thought): Heidegger, Martin: 9780061575594: Amazon.Com: Books."
211   Coffey, "The Whole Rahner on the Supernatural Existential."

will never make philosophy or religion obsolete" (Jun 30, 2020, Ethan Siegel, Forbes Magazine)[212]. Siegel argues correctly that religion deals with questions of the "*why*" (why are we here?), while science asks questions of the "*how*" (how did humans develop?). The *how* questions are technical in nature and require the experimental design of reproducible observations in controlled conditions, such as studying the effects of a certain agent or drug on the contractile function of the heart cells (see above example of heart attack reduction).

The *why* questions are beyond the scope of our current knowledge and understanding and are more sensitive for speculation and thoughts that cannot be proven or disproven with available scientific technologies.

In contrast to the differences between science and religion, there are subtle disparities between philosophy and religion. Different to religion, philosophy tries to answer questions to the why in the absence of authoritative dogmas or religious beliefs, based on reason and logic instead. Of interest, both religion and philosophy have delved into explanatory discussions of unexplainable phenomena (such as how the solar system evolved or how certain living species emerged) that have now been understood and are explained using scientific methodology – at least in part (see above discussion on Darwins' theory of evolution).

While religion needs philosophy, it might not be the case the other way around. Theology depends on philosophical ideas, with the addition of the understanding that all humanity is created by God, thus life and its natural course of any person is created by God, therefore philosophy of life without theology is imperfect. According to Ratzinger (who is considered one of the most prolific and most academic theologians of the 20th century besides Karl Rahner, and later became Pope Benedict XVI), a philosophy of the person that does not take into consideration a theological perspective provides only a partial understanding of the person. Ratzinger demonstrates that philosophical anthropology and theological anthropology as well as metaphysics and history must remain in respective dialogue with each other in order to explain and understand life of the human being.[213]

212   Siegel, "No, Science Will Never Make Philosophy Or Religion Obsolete."
213   Uniwersytet w Białymstoku and Proniewski, "Joseph Ratzinger's Philosophical Theology of the Person."

Despite the existence of humankind since at least several thousands of years, the main bulge of knowledge on nature has been accomplished since the scientific revolution in the 19th century with major developments just within the last 100 years.

Evolution, in particular Darwin's concepts and theory has been heavily criticized by the Catholic Church in the past since it appeared to contradict genesis in the Holy Scripture, if read literally. Siegel further discusses the obvious fact that evolution explains how traits are inherited and how organisms change, adapt and develop.[214] However, science fails to give an explanation on the origin of life in general. The reason why it fails is due to the fact that science is not meant to explain the *why*, since its techniques - even though highly sophisticated in a technical sense - are not sufficient to do so.

Evaluating the prospects of science for immortality research, one need to be reminded that whatever is shown in cell cultures or controlled animal experiments with regard to anti-aging and anti-senescence or regeneration cannot be and should not be simply extrapolated to man in general.

Even if a drug, such as shown for the antidiabetic drug *metformin,* might prolong life in an experimental setting in mice, it is currently studied but not proven thus far in humans. Even if it would be reproduced in a clinical trial in humans, that does not automatically mean that every person who takes the drug will live forever (or for a long time).

The advances in medical sciences regarding anti-aging will take many years to decades to be anywhere close to human use to be applied to a broader population. No matter how many anti-aging remedies one make take every day (Ray Kurzweil, the prominent futurist, stated in an interview recently that he is taking more than 90 supplements per day), so far, no human being has ever escaped death.

Realistically, from a basic researcher's perspective, medicine and biotechnology will further advance and humans will be able to combat heart and cardiovascular diseases and hopefully cancer with resulting prolongation of life and survival of current incurable illnesses. Life then can be extended to 120-150 years, as long as regenerative medicine will provide anti-aging

---

214   Siegel, "No, Science Will Never Make Philosophy Or Religion Obsolete."

mechanisms as well as replacement of damaged organ parts. Based on the rapidity of the current progress in research, this most likely can be achieved within the coming 50 years.

A complete transformation to something more durable than current humankind such as even *transhumanistic* states might take several centuries, assuming that the world as it is currently, still exists and has not been destroyed by climate changes (which might be closer than we imagine), human induced disasters such as nuclear wars (which is becoming again, a constant thread nowadays after some ease following the cold war period) or meteorite collisions (which appears for large asteroids (>5km diameter) approximately once every 20 million years). There are other threats to humankind in general and to the individual in particular despite the advances of modern medicine that will likely lead to major breakthroughs in the coming years.

In his popular book "The book of Immortality" Adam Leith Gollner starts the introduction to 400 pages on "*The science, belief, and magic behind living forever*" with the statement "*Immortality doesn't actually exist. ...It resides in thought but not in reality*" and further, "*No examples of anything immortal have ever been found by science*".[215] Even the immortal jellyfish is not really immortal since it is a frail structure, vulnerable to outside aggressors or trauma that can lead to its death, despite its ability to regenerate itself. In Gollner's opinion, the concept of immortality basically emerged from the natural human fear of dying and the lack of knowledge and rational comprehension of what will happen after our lives on earth or after we die. In that sense, science can only explore the knowing, while belief and faith is how we approach what lacks any material or reproducible evidence.

According to the viewpoint of many secularists and atheists, biology should be cogitated like computer software. If accepted accordingly, then everything in biology must be capable to be reprogrammed. Computer sciences in our times demonstrate an exponential rather than a linear development, according to the well-known futurist Ray Kurzweil. In 2005, Kurzweil predicted that comput-

---

215   Gollner, *The Book of Immortality.*

ers will be able to overtake the human brain's abilities - which he described as *singularity* - by the year 2045 (*"The Singularity is Near"*).[216]

Recently, with the rapid advancement of artificial intelligence and quantum computing however, this might be much more imminent, Kurzweil's updated book on singularity (*"The Singularity is Nearer"*) is expected to come out in late 2023.[217]

Without any doubts, electronic engines such as computers will be able to perform activities with higher speed and accuracy than ever before. However, they will not be able to provide what religion does provide to humankind since thousands of years such as faith, help, support, community, strength, and definitely not everlasting life for any human being.

For the public, it is almost impossible to critically evaluate all about the future of life and all the hype about immortality. In contrast to advertising from salespeople for life enhancing products to populistic promises to futuristic theorists including the concepts of transhumanism in which future generations will be a combination of man and machine, or biologic brain activity and microchips, scientific evidence and modern technology will allow prolongation of human life, likely to 120-150 years within a few decades, as long as other natural disasters such as extreme climate changes, viral pandemics such as COVID-19 or a meteorite collision do not abolish all human and earthly efforts.

Immortality on earth, meaning an endless existence of the human species by means of self-regeneration will not be feasible. While anti-aging medicine will provide the means for improved quality of life, survival of catastrophic diseases and appropriate therapies for chronic progressive illnesses, immortality research is not going anywhere in any realistic future.

So far, every human who ever lived on earth did die, and every human who currently lives on earth is going to die, no matter what efforts, financial means, supplements of exercise regimen one might adopt. Even God's son, Jesus Christ, sent by the father to the world, died on the cross for all human

---

216   Kurzweil, *The Singularity Is Near.*
217   "The Singularity Is Nearer - by Ray Kurzweil (Hardcover)."

beings. But he raised on the third day to the side of the holy father for ever-lasting life in heaven.

There is no science that can prevent death completely, there is no technology which can defy death in its totality. Moreover, there is no scientific technology that will ever show us what is going to happen after death. The mystery of our existence and the mystery of life and death, the reason for our being and our consciousness remains the incomprehensible realm of God's creation and our faith in God and an eternal life. The power and the mystery of this faith is the energy which never can be achieved by sciences is what keeps us going, helps us in sadness, desolation and in grief, and stimulates us to exist, to believe, and to love. Of interest, one might argue that medicine and faith comes together in the person of Jesus Christ.

> *There is one physician, of flesh and of spirit, originate and*
> *unoriginate, God in man, true Life in death, son of Mary and*
> *son of God, first passible and then impassible: Jesus Christ our Lord.*
> Ignatius of Antioch

Ignatius here called Jesus a physician, while others speak of the divine doctor (Matt Emerson 2014).[218]

Until future technologies might develop more advances in defying diseases or even beyond these possibilities, advances in technology, science and modern medicine do not contradict one's faith in an everlasting existence of the soul or resurrection of the human being after our natural death.

In my opinion as a medical researcher, a physician and a Roman Catholic theologian, the promising advances in medicine and technology to prolong life do not replace or contradict the need and the power of faith and religion. Faith is as old as human nature and is – in fact – constant and everlasting, while the biologic sciences are relatively new and are constantly changing the world.

---

218   "Christ as Divine Physician."

Chapter Thirty-Eight

Recommendations for Health Care Practice and Education

For physicians and health care providers the constant struggle between personal faith (if any) and trust in science and modern medicine might be challenging, in particular in situations of dealing with chronic incurable diseases such as cancer and heart failure or in end-of life care circumstances. Providing maximal care on one site – even though technically feasible – might not always be in the best interest for the current well-being and quality of life and graceful dying of an individual patient.[219]

---

219 Schwarz et al., "Maximal Care Considerations When Treating Patients with End-Stage Heart Failure," December 2011. moral, psychological and medico-legal challenge for health care providers. Especially in patients with chronic heart failure, the ethical and medico-legal issues associated with providing maximal possible care or withholding the same are coming to the forefront. Procedures, such as cardiac transplantation, have strict criteria for adequate candidacy. These criteria for subsequent listing are based on clinical outcome data but also reflect the reality of organ shortage. Lack of compliance and non-adherence to lifestyle changes represent relative contraindications to heart transplant candidacy. Mechanical circulatory support therapy using ventricular assist devices is becoming a more prominent therapeutic option for patients with end-stage heart failure who are not candidates for transplantation, which also requires strict criteria to enable beneficial outcome for the patient. Physicians need to critically reflect that in many cases, the patient's best interest might not always mean pursuing maximal technological options available. This article reflects on the multitude of critical issues that health care providers have to face while caring for patients with end-stage heart failure.","container-title":"Journal of Religion and Health","DOI":"10.1007/s10943-010-9326-y","ISSN":"1573-6571","issue":"4","journ alAbbreviation":"J Relig Health","language":"eng","note":"PMID: 20191322\nPMCID: PMC3230758","page":"872-879","source":"PubMed","title":"Maximal care considerations when treating patients with end-stage heart failure: ethical and procedural quandaries in management of the very sick","title-short":"Maximal care considerations when treating patients with end-stage heart failure","volume":"50","author":[{"family":"Schwarz","given":"Ernst R."},{"family":"Philip","given":"Kiran J."},{"family":"Simsir","given":"Sinan A."},{"family":"Czer","given":"Lawrence"},{"family":"Trento","given":"Alfredo"},{"family":"Finder","given":"Stuart

The health care provider has to recognize and accept the limitations of technical and instrumental medicine once it is considered futile. Even more, prolongation of organic function by maintaining a vegetative state in patients with irreversible brain damage might be not the wish of many if there is no realistic prospects for any improvement. Instead, comfort care measures as part of palliative care might be more appropriate to alleviate suffering, at least in certain cases.

In addition, several studies have confirmed that spirituality and religious beliefs are associated with reduced morbidity and mortality, improved coping skills and improved quality of life. [220,221] Our own group demonstrated that even visits by religious clergy and prayers do positively affect length of hospital stay and outcomes in patients with chronic heart failure.[222] Despite the enormous advances in modern medicine and its effects on prolongation of life and improvement of symptoms, diseases are often affecting the entire individual rather than just one organ system. As such, the experience of illnesses goes hand in hand with arising questions of the meaning of life and death. The trust in the medical profession and an empathic doctor-patient relationship with effective communication is a pre-requisite for quality of health care.

Several choices about medical treatments should be done as a *shared decision* between health care providers and patients, based on their personal wishes and goals. Spirituality has been accepted as an important factor in the holistic care of any patient and therefore, should be addressed accordingly. [223]

The question is, however, if a physician should address the patients' faith or spirituality directly. It might appear that patients want to see their doctor

G."},{"family":"Cleenewerck","given":"Laurent A."}]},"issued":{"date-parts":[["2011",12]]}}}],"schema":"https://github.com/citation-style-language/schema/raw/master/csl-citation.json"}

220   King and Bushwick, "Beliefs and Attitudes of Hospital Inpatients about Faith Healing and Prayer."37% wanted their physicians to discuss religious beliefs with them more frequently, and 48% wanted their physicians to pray with them. However, 68% said their physician had never discussed religious beliefs with them.\nCONCLUSIONS: This study supports the hypothesis that although many patients desire more frequent and more in-depth discussions about religious issues with their physicians, physicians generally do not discuss these issues with their patients.","container-title":"The Journal of Family Practice","ISSN":"0094-3509","issue":"4","journalAbbreviation":"J Fam Pract","language":"eng","note":"PMID: 7931113","page":"349-352","source":"PubMed","title":"Beliefs and attitudes of hospital inpatients about faith healing and prayer","volume":"39","author":[{"family":"King","given":"D. E."},{"family":"Bushwick","given":"B."}],"issued":{"date-parts":[["1994",10]]}}],"schema":"https://github.com/citation-style-language/schema/raw/master/csl-citation.json"}

221   Levin, Larson, and Puchalski, "Religion and Spirituality in Medicine."
222   Naghi et al., "The Effects of Spirituality and Religion on Outcomes in Patients with Chronic Heart Failure."
223   Pulciani and Nutile, "[Relationships between Medicine and Spirituality]."

as a professional healer rather than a spiritual advisor and therefore, might consider it inappropriate for a health care provider to bring up faith, which could seem like saying "this is all we can offer", and some atheists might think so. Patients might want the physician being their helper *here and now* and not someone who talks about the '*thereafter*'. Even though this might be true for some, several studies have demonstrated that the vast majority of patients, however, do welcome a discussion of religion and spirituality in medical consultations. [224]

Based on our research we strongly believe that a multidisciplinary approach to enable a healthy patient provider relationship should include addressing issues of faith as part of a holistic care. As such, I might even go further to recommend the introduction of *Theologic Medicine* into the curriculum of the studies of medicine at teaching institutions.

Even though a detailed excursion of my proposed *Faculty of Theologic Medicine* would be beyond the frame of the current book, I summarize in brief the proposal. In this context, *Theologic Medicine* should not be confused with the term *Medical Theology*, which was proposed in 1900 but has not been implemented into any curriculum, as far as we know. [225]

Theologic Medicine would and should incorporate the following 10 aspects:

1. Inclusion of the patient's faith, wishes and goals into the therapeutic management of acute and chronic disease, in a sense similiar to the inclusion of palliative care in the therapy of heart failure or cancer. In this context, it needs to be emphasized that palliative

---

224   Best, Butow, and Olver, "Do Patients Want Doctors to Talk about Spirituality?"
225   "MEDICAL THEOLOGY."to be thinking of founding a course on medical theology in Laval University. Our contemporary does not know just what medical theology is, but hopes that it may not be added to the already overburdened curriculum of the student. The term is new to us also, but if we may venture a guess, we would think the course might include certain questions of medical deontology such as those arising in connection with abortion, baptism, etc., which have been more or less extensively discussed by Roman Catholic theologians. The medical profession has generally held that the proper application of the recognized ethical principles is sufficient for all emergencies, but there are still some doctrinal points on which the church may deem some special instruction required, and that will also come within the compass of the proposed course. This is offered","container-title":"Journal of the American Medical Association","DOI":"10.1001/jama.1900.02460170055012","ISSN":"0002-9955","issue":"17","journalAb breviation":"Journal of the American Medical Association","page":"1075","source":"Silverchair","title":"MEDICAL THEOLOGY.","URL":"https://doi.org/10.1001/jama.1900.02460170055012","volume":"XXXIV","accessed":{"date-part s":[["2022",2,4]]},"issued":{"date-parts":[["1900",4,28]]}}}],"schema":"https://github.com/citation-style-language/schema/raw/master/csl-citation.json"}

care is not identical to hospice care, which deals with end-of life, while palliative care deals with the incurable diseases that still can be ongoing for years. In this context, faith is not only important for end-of life situations but for the entire processes of disease, treatment, healing, and coping.

2. As discussed in the current book, the ideas of immortality in a secular natural or biologic context as well as everlasting or eternal life in a religious sense especially in view of patient expectations and reality of medical care that can be provided without becoming futile should be critically evaluated and discussed by the health care provider in order to present a holistic but realistic medical care while also providing psychological and spiritual support - either directly or by use of specially trained team members.

3. The teachings of a compassionate co-existence of science and religion as well as the acceptance of scientific facts that do not negate anyone's personal faith, in contrast to traditional notions of controversies between biblical texts and scientific discoveries by encouragement of hermeneutic interpretation of exegetical understandings and allegorical rather than literal reading of sacred scriptures.

4. The acceptance and ecumenical cooperation of different religions and religious communities for the social, ethical, spiritual and psychological support of the ill.

5. The implementation of "*Notfallseelsorge*", which can be translated to spiritual or pastoral *crisis intervention* using pastoral theology and psychology during community catastrophic events such as earthquakes or terroristic attacks or during war to provide spiritual welfare as an integral part of emergency care activities, but also in individual cases of emergencies such as sudden life changes caused by disease or accidents.

6. The routine support of spiritual care at end-of life situations for the individual patients but also the care givers and families to help with processes of acceptance of incurable conditions and of dying, and to deal with death with dignity.

7. The spiritual and pastoral involvement in supporting the processes of grief and coping guidance for family members before, at the time of and after the death of a loved one.

8. In addition, the delivery of spiritual support for health care providers to cope with the enormous psychological and physical stressors of taking care for the very sick, not limited to but also in situations such as the overwhelming working hours during the current COVID-19 pandemic in emergency department and intensive care units or even in skilled nursing homes with facing death and despair of helplessness on one hand while being overworked until exhaustion on the other hand, including its bearing on personal lives and families of health care providers.

9. The inclusion of bioethics into the training program in order to provide health care providers with information of ethical issues arising from advances in modern medicine and technology but also to teach moral requirements to perform responsible research and medical care with appropriateness and integrity for the best individual care of patients, for the environment, and for public health.

10. The addition of medical ethics (supplemental and somehow overlapping with bioethics) to assist the provider to deal with moral values and respect for autonomy, beneficence, nonmaleficence, and justice in the practice of medicine, especially in cases of decision making for or against therapies, in cases where patients or a power of attorney might not be able to make decisions, in cases of non-escalation of care or withdrawal of care, initiation of comfort care or DNR orders (do not resuscitate), or even in cases of limited medical resource allocation in situations of major disasters (who should get treatment if only few but not all can).

A curriculum in Theologic Medicine would require appropriate initial training for health care providers by experienced physicians and nursing staff, spiritual advisors, clergy representatives such as pastors or priests from different churches or faith communities, bioethicists, psychologists, social workers, psychotherapists, patient support group members, members of institutional review boards, researchers, and even legal advisors. Maintenance for attendance of re-fresher teaching courses and subsequent evaluation of competency in Theologic Medicine should then be continued throughout the professional career in health care.

Chapter Thirty-Nine

The Metaverse Immortality

A s astonishing it might sound, the metaverse is not something in the future, but it is already here. Man can buy land in the metaverse, virtual land, and there is already a bid going on the get virtual properties, which are limited of course, so that it is worth to fight for it. What is the *metaverse*?

Facebook's CEO Mark Zuckerberg (born 1984) announced in 2021 that *Facebook* is changing its brand to *meta* in order to play the major role in the next big thing after the explosion of the internet in the 90s.

The metaverse is basically virtual reality in its finest, which as per futurists and business advocates, will definitely take over the role of the internet for all portions of our human life, whether it is social, personal, spiritual or business life, even more than the world wide web did three decades ago.

Let us understand how this came about and then we will indulge into the virtual immortality, which is quite different from anything such as natural or biologic immortality but opens clearly another world for us and our dependents in the future, as long as the earth might still exist.

Let us go back to the beginning of the internet. The internet is a network of networks, basically a global system that interconnected computer networks, enabling everyone on earth who has internet access to connect to all whatever has been posted on internet websites. As a communication tool, the U.S Department of Defense developed what was called ARPANET in the 1960s, the *Advanced Research Projects Agency Network*, which was an invention that was based on ideas of brilliant minds such as Nicola Tesla, who in the 1900s came up with the idea of a worldwide wireless system, whereas others proposed mechanized searchable storage systems for books and media in the 1930s. The ARPANET used a method called "packet switching" to allow electronic data being transmitted to allow multiple computers to communicate on a single network platform. This allowed researchers or institutions initially to conduct a *time sharing* of information at different computer locations in order to protect sensitive data if one site would have been destroyed by a nuclear war, which was the main fear during the cold war between the US and the NATO on one site and the Soviet Union (UDSSR) on the other site – which is a similar situation now in 2022 as a result of Russia's unlawful invasion of Ukraine.

At the time of the cold war, computers were very large machines confined to one location. The first attempt to transfer a message weas conducted by Leonard Kleinrock at my home institution UCLA in 1965 when he sent a message to a computer in Stanford. By 1973, 30 academic, military and research institutions had joined the network in the US and Europe. As a result of these initial efforts to compromise and transfer data between computers, smaller and cheaper desktop computers were developed which then allowed the development of local area networks, and then two researchers at the University of Southern California (my other former home institution) invented the *Domain Name System* which then let Tim Berners Lee from CERN (the international particle research laboratory in Geneva, Switzerland) develop the *world-wide web*. The internet today is an unlimited source of information, a base for electronic communication (email), and a communication tool through shared information space for personal use, business and especially for social media.

It is almost incomprehensible for today's youngsters how our generation grew up without internet and without cell phones. I remember using a public phone in the midst of the village with saved coins to call a girl from school as a teenager before we had our first own house phone.

Later, when I worked at the Max Planck Institute for Experimental Research at the world renowned Kerckhoff Institute for Experimental and Clinical Physiology, I bought my first personal computer in 1990, but I had no idea what to do with it. My colleagues told me about writing programs, and I thought, what the heck am I supposed to do with a writing program and what am I supposed to write all day long? So, I started writing summaries of research papers that I read to create my first electronic bibliography.

When I then came to the US to work in a research laboratory at the University of Southern California in Los Angeles in 1991, I used for the first time the email that was assigned to me from the RWTH University of Technology in Aachen, Germany, to communicate with my colleagues from Germany. To my very surprise, none of my US American coworkers who all were cardiology fellows, had any idea what email was at that time, or even how to turn on a desktop computer. At that time, the internet was already formed, which stands for Interconnected Network, and I remember that each international conference of the American Heart Association or the American College of Cardiology that I attended every year to give lectures had learning sessions for internet use that were usually packed, mainly by Europeans. At the same time, I had my first smart phone, a flip phone of the size of an adult men's shoe, which I used proudly driving my convertible on Sunset Boulevard in Los Angeles. The first smart phone that I saw ever was actually an old-fashioned phone that looked like a house rotary phone and was shown to me by a Japanese cardiology researcher after a conference in Kobe, Japan, during drinking sake and singing Karaoke.

Years later, when I visited a conference in China, I had 2 cell phones, an I-phone and a Blackberry, but at that time none worked during my one-week trip to China, and I was in heaven: no calls, no texts, no emails for an entire week, I felt free.

Upon my return to the US, however, it took me over a week to catch up with the 30,000 calls, messages, emails and requests that suddenly were uploaded over a few hours after I landed back in Los Angeles.

Imagine a world nowadays without cell phones, laptops or the web: that would be unthinkable and disastrous for basically almost every single business in the world, all scholarly institutions, and most of people's social life.

The *metaverse* is the next big thing after the internet revolution in the 1990s. The metaverse represents a system for artificial intelligence and virtual reality that is supported by platforms that are in development right now. Virtual reality is now considered to be augmented reality and includes everything daily life could offer in a virtual space.

Man can buy land in the metaverse, and people are able to attend parties and go to sit in virtual auditoriums to listen to lectures in the metaverse. Besides its technological and financial opportunities, the demand for a virtual world is even higher than ever since the worldwide COVID pandemic in 2020/2021.

Many businesses changed their practice from in-office presence to work from-home, which is not only cheaper for the businesses, but also more convenient for the individuals. Imagine not needing to leave your house ever again since you can work from home, have conferences per ZOOM meetings, attend exercise sessions online, and go to have a drink and dance in the metaverse. This prospective might make life easier for many (think about single moms taking care for their kids at home but still now being able to work from home for several hours rather than spending hours in an office building away from home), and it could provide the benefits of avoiding any individual, social, geographic or timely limitations that make life harder or sometimes even impossible.

On the other hand, the risks of real social isolation and loss of sense of reality might create long term issues not imaginable at this point in time, some believe that its anthropomorphisms might be a possibility for black sheep to create intentional conflicts, its easy immersiveness could result in addiction to simulated reality in which some might just live only in the metaverse rather than in a real world, subsequent mental health issues, antisocial behaviors, spending sprees, and privacy issues, among many many others.

On the other hand, as it developed for the internet that started 30 years ago, there are almost unlimited possibilities for nosiness and education and worldwide connectivity. My personal take is that the metaverse likely will host virtual hospitals and medical office clinics patients can visit at any time for consultations and treatment - without any waiting periods.

Bedsides this, the metaverse can definitely create virtual immortality for anyone, since it is going to provide a reality in an alternate world that can renew and regenerate itself limitless. The metaverse is already using the so-called Web3 technology enabled through blockchain possibilities as utilized for cryptocurrencies and NFTs (non-fungible tokens). According to a recently posted report on the web an author mentioned that "*there are digital immortality cryptos such as the metaverse versus biologic immortality cryptos such medical sciences and research (stem cell) cryptos*".[226]

Even though it is somewhat ominous, cryptocurrencies seem to life in a virtual reality already. It appears obvious that a virtual reality can easily create any currency, any fantasy, and even everlasting life at any developmental stage for any individual.

Even though there is no death in the metaverse (I guess, unless in a criminal or sinister reality that intends to hurt the avatar), it is a fact that not using the metaverse will result in cessation of your existence, you will be out – and dead. If you are biologically dead in real life, you obviously cannot use the metaverse anymore, and you are therefore virtually dead, too.

For this reason, metaverse users in the near future might be able to create themselves immortal in whatever stage, age and appearance they wish to do so, within the virtual environment, possibly to be seen by and communicated with by their real family members and friends after their earthly death (if they still have a family and friends in the real world, which might be a reasonable concern).

In the same way as virtual land is offered for sale in the metaverse, sooner or later one can buy his or her everlasting existence in the virtual world, the price might depend on appearance and status as well as on accessibility for others, so you might get an immortality life in your village community or in direct neighborhood to adjacent virtual land plots, or you might buy immortality for the next 100,000 years for worldwide accessibility to be part of sev-

---

226   Brainwashed99, "Digital Immortality (Metaverse) vs. Biological Immortality (Stem Cells) Cryptos."

eral realities (from car race participations to nightclubs to family gatherings among thousands of others). The metaverse can then use your user profile over the last used periods to create your immortal avatar, even without your participation. This virtual life after death, of course represents pure digital rather than biologic immortality, and let us just hope that neither the internet in its entirety nor the metaverse will ever be hacked worldwide in a way that no one could use it anymore, that would create a universal personal, societal, social and economic disaster.

Virtual immortality at its current stage is more part of a game or a toy with enormous potential for education and arts, but it has nothing to do with biologic immortality or with the Christian belief in the resurrection after death.

Chapter Fourty

My Personal Critical Thoughts

I n today's world, there is hardly any room for religion and faith in our post-modern societies. Daily life is pre-occupied with learning, studying, and work and dreams that are about wealth and accumulation of materialistic goods and professional acceptance, success and power, while social life predominantly is shifting towards online activities, which creates addiction that abolishes time to reflect, to think or to create. Instead of creating artistic or intellectual content, many are just lost in passivity that is supported by senseless observation of reels, 20 second Tiktok videos and unsophisticated communication via Instagram or telegram. That is like watching lions killing gladiators in the ancient Rome (*panem et circenses*, bread and games, or like going to the casinos in Las Vegas or elsehwere), for easily satisfiable passive amusement.

Our upbringing– at least in the Western world - was targeted towards a good education, earning academic degrees, and subsequent to that, getting jobs to be able to afford having a family and a home. The higher the education, usually the better the professional opportunities and the higher the salaries are (that is how I grew up in Germany).

Religion was something for the grandparents who did or did not go to Church on Sundays but had no role in our secularized world. Only few of my peers in school or later at the University had even heard of or had read about Kierkegaard or Martin Heidegger, and even less about Thomas Aquinas or St. Augustine, even though I was indulging in reading philosophy and theology as an attempt to understand life in my teens.

I don't think my 20 and 22year old daughters have ever heard any of these names. While I was spending most of my childhood outdoors hunting foxes and wolves (hunting in watching but not killing them), the next generation spent most of their time watching TV, whereas today's kids seem to spend most of their time and efforts on social media and suffer accordingly since it might become a disaster if somehow someone posted something about someone. Mental health issues, bullying, social acceptance issues and isolation might occur, even suicidal ideation has been reported.

The way kids grow up in the Western world, in particular in the United States, is quite different nowadays. Even though the educational system is still focused on higher education as the goal for a successful professional career, the world shows us every day that individuals can become unbelievably rich without any education, from being a dish washer to a millionaire as an actor or an actress in the late 60s, then from living on the streets to become a rapper selling millions of songs in the early 90s, then becoming billionaires by inventing a social media platform in the early 2000, and now people make money be trading vague cyptocurrencies using their cell phones from home, which requires nothing more than understanding the platform and some luck by investing correctly. I know individuals who make between $ 1,000 and 10,000 per day by spending a few hours online, whereas others work their butts off in doing hard labor in construction or cleaning hospital bathrooms for $14 per hour ($112 per day), while some doctors work in hospitals and clinics taking care for indigenous people 14 hours per day with minimal payments.

There must be something wrong in the system, if hard work, ambition and good education does not pay off, anymore, at least if compared to the above examples.

Our daily activity level is constantly on high alert and our schedules are packed with minute slots that are assigned for certain tasks, which does hardly allow any time to relax (accept falling deadly asleep secondary to exhaustion at the end of the day), to regroup, to think, to be creative or foster our fantasies, or even to pray.

Does this create happiness in life? I am sure that at one point, everyone might come to a conclusion that it does not, oftentimes at a point in life when the energy train does not ride in the predetermined direction or loses its speed, for example when something unexpected happened, such as a disease or an accident or an outside disaster that changes the individual's world from one day to another.

It is easier said than done, but in today's busy life, we must not forget to reconsider our purpose, take time to meditate, to think, to enjoy the simplest things in life, and to think about the coming after our earthly existence, which despite hoarding cryptocurrencies or getting space in the metaverse, is limited for all of us, as it has been forever.

Chapter Forty-One

Conclusion

In summary, philosophy deals with an everlasting soul after cessation of the earthly existence, going back to Plato. In Christianity, an immortal soul – even though never mentioned in the Scriptures – according to Thomas Aquinas, is what gives the person (or animal, or plant) the spirit of life and therefore, is immortal.

Even though death is the final cessation of all bodily function, the Christian faith centers around the resurrection of man after death to be existent in heaven in a divine-like state.

Biological sciences, on the other hand, attempt to counteract the processes of aging and death by re-programming cells from undergoing senescent changes to everlasting regeneration. Stem cell therapy as the mainstay for regeneration is supposed to help to overcome organ dysfunction as a result of degenerative age-related changes or diseases, with huge advances and promising results in preclinical and clinical studies.

This work outlines the different aspects of immortality from a philosophical aspect to a Christian view to the scientific background and to the populistic view how to gain ever-lasting human existence.

From a scientific point of view, modern medicine and biotechnology will likely help to prolong life beyond the current average 70-80 years of age towards 100s, 120s and beyond within the next 50 years. Whether or not immortality will be achieved within the next 100 or 200 years or even beyond, is very much unlikely.

A life prolongation on the other hand, will be achievable with a prolonged health span, which in turn can then result in increased socio-economic productivity and quality of a longer life with maintained functionality, as long as societies will be prepared to take care for much larger older populations.

At the current time, the only way to avoid aging is - dying. On the other hand, age is the number one risk factor for death. Every day, approximately 100,000 people die of aging. Due to our research on clinical studies the elixir for long lasting life can be stem cell therapy and genetic re-programming of cellular aging processes, whereas the key to immortality remains in our faith of resurrection after death with eternal life in a realm beyond our limited understanding.

Science and faith do not contradict each other, science helps us to understand, faith keeps us around. The hallmark of science is that it changes all the time, while faith is immortal, as evidenced by thousands of years.

The implementation of theologic approaches into medicine can be supplemental to the armamentarium of health care providers to enable a holistic and ethical sound approach to the management of patients with incurable diseases.

Acknowledgment

I would like to acknowledge the continuous and inspiring support and guidance of Professor Dr. Laurent Cleenewerck during my studies and in the preparation of this book, our weekly online meetings were a welcoming break in my work as a physician and lead to the transformation to a different intellectual level. Further, I would like to thank my wife Angela for her love, patience and emotional and practical support during this journey and my children Aubriana d'Iwana Angel, Lujain Vanessa, Cecilia Florence Magdalena, Nathaniel Ferdinand Valentino, and Rafferty Atticus Kip for their love and accepting time away from them to accomplish this book.

Bibliography

BBC News. "400-Year-Old Greenland Shark 'Longest-Living Vertebrate,'" August 12, 2016, sec. Science & Environment. https://www.bbc.com/news/science-environment-37047168.

Adventures in Immortality by George Gallup, n.d.

"Aquinas 101." Accessed January 13, 2022. https://aquinas101.thomisticinstitute.org/.

Aquinas, Thomas. *The Summa Theologica of St. Thomas Aquinas*. Translated by Fathers of the English Dominican Provinc. English Dominican Province Translation edition. New York: Christian Classics, 1981.

Aristotle. *The Metaphysics*. Translated by Hugh Lawson-Tancred. New Ed edition. London ; New York: Penguin Classics, 1999.

Augustine, Saint. *The Confessions of St. Augustine*. Lulu.com, 1995.

Bailey, Lee W., and Jenny Yates. *The Near-Death Experience: A Reader*. Routledge, 2013.

Balthasar, Hans Urs von. "Easter: He Walked Where There Was No Path." Church Life Journal. Accessed November 24, 2021. https://churchlifejournal.nd.edu/articles/easter-we-walked-where-there-was-no-path/.

Barbour, Ian G. *Issues in Science and Religion*. Englewood Cliffs, N.J.: Prentice-Hall, 1966.

Barbour, Ian G. *Religion and Science.* Revised, Subsequent edition. San Francisco: HarperOne, 1997.

Bauerschmidt, Frederick C., and James J. Buckley. *Catholic Theology: An Introduction.* 1st edition. Wiley-Blackwell, 2016.

Beek, Johannes H. G. M. van, Thomas B. L. Kirkwood, and James B. Bassingthwaighte. "Understanding the Physiology of the Ageing Individual: Computational Modelling of Changes in Metabolism and Endurance." *Interface Focus* 6, no. 2 (April 6, 2016): 20150079. https://doi.org/10.1098/rsfs.2015.0079.

BioLogos. "Behe and Irreducible Complexity: Failure to Engage the Evidence - Articles." Accessed March 31, 2022. https://biologos.org/articles/behe-and-irreducible-complexity-failure-to-engage-the-evidence/.

Behe, Michael J. *A Mousetrap for Darwin: Michael J. Behe Answers His Critics.* Seattle, WA: Discovery Institute, 2020.

———. *Darwin's Black Box: The Biochemical Challenge to Evolution.* 2nd edition. New York: Free Press, 2006.

"Being and Time (Harper Perennial Modern Thought): Heidegger, Martin: 9780061575594: Amazon.Com: Books." Accessed January 19, 2022. https://www.amazon.com/Being-Harper-Perennial-Modern-Thought/dp/0061575593.

Best, Megan, Phyllis Butow, and Ian Olver. "Do Patients Want Doctors to Talk about Spirituality? A Systematic Literature Review." *Patient Education and Counseling* 98, no. 11 (November 2015): 1320–28. https://doi.org/10.1016/j.pec.2015.04.017.

Bigelow, William Sturgis. *Buddhism and Immortality.* CreateSpace Independent Publishing Platform, 2011.

Blagosklonny, Mikhail V. "How to Save Medicare: The Anti-Aging Remedy." *Aging* 4, no. 8 (August 2012): 547–52. https://doi.org/10.18632/aging.100479.

———. "Rapamycin for Longevity: Opinion Article." *Aging* 11, no. 19 (October 4, 2019): 8048–67. https://doi.org/10.18632/aging.102355.

Blumenfeld, Remy. "How A 15,000-Year-Old Human Bone Could Help You Through The Coronacrisis." Forbes. Accessed December 2, 2021.

https://www.forbes.com/sites/remyblumenfeld/2020/03/21/how-a-15000-year-old-human-bone-could-help-you-through-the-coronavirus/.

Borges, Jorge Luis, and Eliot Weinberger. "Immortality." *New England Review (1990-)* 20, no. 3 (1999): 11–16. https://www.jstor.org/stable/40243722.

Brainwashed99. "Digital Immortality (Metaverse) vs. Biological Immortality (Stem Cells) Cryptos." Reddit Post. *R/CryptoCurrency*, December 2, 2021. www.reddit.com/r/CryptoCurrency/comments/r72ngg/digital_immortality_metaverse_vs_biological/.

"Brian Brinzan, The Theory of the Immortality of the Soul with Saint Augustine, the Scientific Journal of Humanistic Studies 5, No 9 (2013), 146.," n.d.

Brooke, John Hedley. "Science, Religion, and Historical Complexity." *Historically Speaking* 8, no. 5 (2007): 10–13. https://doi.org/10.1353/hsp.2007.0028.

Buben, Adam. "The Dark Side of Desire: Nietzsche, Transhumanism, and Personal Immortality." *The Southern Journal of Philosophy* 59, no. 1 (2021): 66–84. https://doi.org/10.1111/sjp.12393.

Buchen, Irving H. "The Ordeal of Richard Feverel: Science Versus Nature." *ELH* 29, no. 1 (1962): 47–66. https://doi.org/10.2307/2871925.

Buettner, Dan, and Sam Skemp. "Blue Zones: Lessons From the World's Longest Lived." *American Journal of Lifestyle Medicine* 10, no. 5 (October 2016): 318–21. https://doi.org/10.1177/1559827616637066.

Burley, Mikel. "Immortality and Meaning: Reflections on the Makropulos Debate: Mikel Burley." *Philosophy* 84, no. 4 (2009): 529–47. https://doi.org/10.1017/S0031819109990106.

Caire, Anne-Blandine. "[Cryogenics]." *Journal International De Bioethique Et D'ethique Des Sciences* 29, no. 3 (December 2018): 54–70. https://doi.org/10.3917/jibes.293.0054.

Callahan, D. "Managed Care and the Goals of Medicine." *Journal of the American Geriatrics Society* 46, no. 3 (March 1998): 385–88. https://doi.org/10.1111/j.1532-5415.1998.tb01060.x.

"Catholics Are Losing Faith in Clergy and Church after Sexual Abuse Scandal, Gallup Survey Says | CNN." Accessed January 17, 2022. https://www.cnn.com/2019/01/11/us/catholic-gallup-survey/index.html.

Cholbi, Michael. "Immortality Project Research Review," n.d., 36.

America Magazine. "Christ as Divine Physician," November 7, 2014. https://www.americamagazine.org/content/ignatian-educator/christ-divine-physician.

Church, Catholic. *Catechism of the Catholic Church: With Modifications from the Editio Typica*. Doubleday, 1997.

Coffey, David. "The Whole Rahner on the Supernatural Existential." *Theological Studies* 65, no. 1 (February 2004): 95–118. https://doi.org/10.1177/004056390406500135.

Cohen, I. Bernard. "The Fear and Distrust of Science in Historical Perspective." *Science, Technology, & Human Values* 6, no. 36 (1981): 20–24. https://www.jstor.org/stable/689095.

Comhaire, Frank, and Wim Decleer. "Can the Biological Mechanisms of Ageing Be Corrected by Food Supplementation. The Concept of Health Care over Sick Care." *The Aging Male: The Official Journal of the International Society for the Study of the Aging Male* 23, no. 5 (December 2020): 1146–57. https://doi.org/10.1080/13685538.2020.1713080.

CORDEIRO, JOSÉ LUIS. "From Biological To Technological Evolution." *World Affairs: The Journal of International Issues* 15, no. 1 (2011): 86–99. https://www.jstor.org/stable/48504845.

Cottingham, John. *The Cambridge Companion to Descartes*. Cambridge University Press, 1992.

Cullmann, Oscar. *Immortality of the Soul or Resurrection of the Dead?: The Witness of the New Testament*. Reprint edition. Wipf & Stock Pub, 2000.

Darwin, Charles. *The Origin of Species*. Beyond Books Hub, 2021.

Dawkins, Richard. *The God Delusion*. Reprint edition. Boston: Mariner Books, 2008.

Devarapalli, Pratap, Ranjith N. Kumavath, Debmalya Barh, and Vasco Azevedo. "The Conserved Mitochondrial Gene Distribution in Relatives of Turritopsis Nutricula, an Immortal Jellyfish." *Bioinformation* 10, no. 9 (2014): 586–91. https://doi.org/10.6026/97320630010586.

Dhanjal, Daljeet Singh, Sonali Bhardwaj, Ruchi Sharma, Kanchan Bhardwaj, Dinesh Kumar, Chirag Chopra, Eugenie Nepovimova, Reena Singh, and Kamil Kuca. "Plant Fortification of the Diet for Anti-Ageing Effects: A Review." *Nutrients* 12, no. 10 (September 30, 2020): E3008. https://doi.org/10.3390/nu12103008.

Dickel, Sascha, and Jan-Felix Schrape. "Dezentralisierung, Demokratisierung, Emanzipation: Zur Architektur Des Digitalen Technikutopismus." *Leviathan* 43, no. 3 (2015): 442–63. https://www.jstor.org/stable/24886305.

St. Mary's Catholic Center. "Did Methuselah Really Live 969 Years?" Accessed January 12, 2022. https://www.aggiecatholic.org/blog/2013/09/did-methuselah-really-live-969-years.

Dixon, Dougal. *After Man: A Zoology of the Future.* 1st edition. New York; Godalming: St. Martin's Griffin, 1998.

Dzobo, Kevin, Nicholas Ekow Thomford, Dimakatso Alice Senthebane, Hendrina Shipanga, Arielle Rowe, Collet Dandara, Michael Pillay, and Keolebogile Shirley Caroline M. Motaung. "Advances in Regenerative Medicine and Tissue Engineering: Innovation and Transformation of Medicine." *Stem Cells International* 2018 (2018): 2495848. https://doi.org/10.1155/2018/2495848.

Ecklund, Elaine Howard, David R. Johnson, Christopher P. Scheitle, Kirstin R. W. Matthews, and Steven W. Lewis. "Religion among Scientists in International Context: A New Study of Scientists in Eight Regions." *Socius* 2 (January 1, 2016): 2378023116664353. https://doi.org/10.1177/2378023116664353.

Edgar, L., T. Pu, B. Porter, J. M. Aziz, C. La Pointe, A. Asthana, and G. Orlando. "Regenerative Medicine, Organ Bioengineering and Transplantation." *The British Journal of Surgery* 107, no. 7 (June 2020): 793–800. https://doi.org/10.1002/bjs.11686.

Ehman, J. W., B. B. Ott, T. H. Short, R. C. Ciampa, and J. Hansen-Flaschen. "Do Patients Want Physicians to Inquire about Their

Spiritual or Religious Beliefs If They Become Gravely Ill?" *Archives of Internal Medicine* 159, no. 15 (August 9, 1999): 1803–6. https://doi.org/10.1001/archinte.159.15.1803.

EISDORFER, CARL. "ON THE PROLONGATION OF LIFE." *Gerontology / היגולוטנורג*, no. 8 (1978): 4–8. https://www.jstor.org/stable/23479532.

Eissenberg, Joel C. "Hungering for Immortality." *Missouri Medicine* 115, no. 1 (February 2018): 12–17.

Elmore, Susan. "Apoptosis: A Review of Programmed Cell Death." *Toxicologic Pathology* 35, no. 4 (June 2007): 495–516. https://doi.org/10.1080/01926230701320337.

Eschatology: Death and Eternal Life, Edition 0002. Accessed November 24, 2021. https://www.christianbook.com/eschatology-death-eternal-life-edition-0002/joseph-ratzinger/9780813215167/pd/215167.

Facebook, Twitter, Show more sharing options, Facebook, Twitter, LinkedIn, Email, Copy Link URLCopied!, and Print. "Evolution Is More Than a Theory, Pope Tells Scientists." Los Angeles Times, October 25, 1996. https://www.latimes.com/archives/la-xpm-1996-10-25-mn-57403-story.html.

———. "Pope Takes Inclusive View of Salvation." Los Angeles Times, December 9, 2000. https://www.latimes.com/archives/la-xpm-2000-dec-09-me-63282-story.html.

Faria, Miguel A. "Longevity and Compression of Morbidity from a Neuroscience Perspective: Do We Have a Duty to Die by a Certain Age?" *Surgical Neurology International* 6 (2015): 49. https://doi.org/10.4103/2152-7806.154273.

Farman, Abou. *On Not Dying: Secular Immortality in the Age of Technoscience.* University of Minnesota Press, 2020. https://doi.org/10.5749/j.ctv10rrc6z.

Farmer, Linda L. "Straining the Limits of Philosophy: Aquinas on the Immortality of the Human Soul." *Faith and Philosophy* 20, no. 2 (2003): 208–17. https://doi.org/faithphil200320233.

pdfcoffee.com. "Feuerbach - Thoughts on Death and Immortality." Accessed January 18, 2022. https://pdfcoffee.com/feuerbach-thoughts-on-death-and-immortality-pdf-free.html.

Fischer, John Martin. "Immortality." The Oxford Handbook of Philosophy of Death, December 3, 2012. https://doi.org/10.1093/oxfordhb/9780195388923.013.0016.

Fischer, John Martin, and Benjamin Mitchell-Yellin. "Immortality and Boredom." *The Journal of Ethics* 18, no. 4 (2014): 353–72. https://www.jstor.org/stable/43895884.

FLEMING, DONALD. *John William Draper and the Religion of Science.* University of Pennsylvania Press, 1950. https://www.jstor.org/stable/j.ctv5134fn.

Fontinell, Eugene. "Immortality: A Pragmatic-Processive Model." In *Self, God and Immortality*, 200–218. A Jamesian Investigation. Fordham University Press, 2000. https://doi.org/10.2307/j.ctvh4zh07.14.

———. "Immortality: Hope or Hindrance?" In *Self, God and Immortality*, 165–99. A Jamesian Investigation. Fordham University Press, 2000. https://doi.org/10.2307/j.ctvh4zh07.13.

"Foundations of Christian Faith: An Introduction to the Idea of Christianity Karl Rahner and William V. Dych by Karl Rahner: New (1978) | BennettBooksLtd." Accessed November 24, 2021. https://www.abebooks.com/Foundations-Christian-Faith-introduction-idea-Christianity/30892429785/bd.

Frey, Thomas. "DEMYSTIFYING THE FUTURE: The Singularity and Our Collision Path With the Future." *Journal of Environmental Health* 77, no. 1 (2014): 38–39. https://www.jstor.org/stable/26330078.

Fukuyama, Francis. "Transhumanism." *Foreign Policy*, no. 144 (2004): 42–43. https://doi.org/10.2307/4152980.

Gardiner, D., S. Shemie, A. Manara, and H. Opdam. "International Perspective on the Diagnosis of Death." *BJA: British Journal of Anaesthesia* 108, no. suppl_1 (January 1, 2012): i14–28. https://doi.org/10.1093/bja/aer397.

Ghayas, Saba, and Syeda Shahida Batool. "Construction and Validation of Afterlife Belief Scale for Muslims." *Journal of Religion and Health* 56, no. 3 (June 2017): 861–75. https://doi.org/10.1007/s10943-016-0258-z.

Gollner, Adam Leith. *The Book of Immortality.* Doubleday Canada, 2013.

Time. "Google vs. Death." Accessed December 2, 2021. https://time. com/574/google-vs-death/.

Gorzoni, Milton Luiz, and Sueli Luciano Pires. "[Is there any scientific evidence supporting antiaging medicine?]." *Anais Brasileiros De Dermatologia* 85, no. 1 (February 2010): 57–64. https://doi.org/10.1590/s0365-05962010000100008.

"Greek Medicine - The Hippocratic Oath." Exhibitions. U.S. National Library of Medicine. Accessed December 2, 2021. https://www.nlm. nih.gov/hmd/greek/greek_oath.html.

Guidotti, Tee L. "Between Distrust of Science and Scientism." *Archives of Environmental & Occupational Health* 72, no. 5 (September 3, 2017): 247–48. https://doi.org/10.1080/19338244.2017.1312987.

Hawkins, Peter S. "Lost and Found: The Bible and Its Literary Afterlife." *Religion & Literature* 36, no. 1 (2004): 1–14. https://www.jstor.org/stable/40059939.

Helmy, Karim Y., Shyam A. Patel, Kimberly Silverio, Lillian Pliner, and Pranela Rameshwar. "Stem Cells and Regenerative Medicine: Accomplishments to Date and Future Promise." *Therapeutic Delivery* 1, no. 5 (November 2010): 693–705. https://doi.org/10.4155/tde.10.57.

Herranz, Nicolás, and Jesús Gil. "Mechanisms and Functions of Cellular Senescence." *The Journal of Clinical Investigation* 128, no. 4 (April 2, 2018): 1238–46. https://doi.org/10.1172/JCI95148.

Hollands, Edmund H. Review of *Review of Buddhism and Immortality*, by William Sturgis Bigelow. *The Philosophical Review* 18, no. 3 (1909): 346–47. https://doi.org/10.2307/2177881.

Hook, C. Christopher, and Paul S. Mueller. "The Terri Schiavo Saga: The Making of a Tragedy and Lessons Learned." *Mayo Clinic Proceedings* 80, no. 11 (November 1, 2005): 1449–60. https://doi.org/10.4065/80.11.1449.

HOOPLE, ROSS E. "ON IMMORTALITY." *Christian Education* 15, no. 5 (1932): 310–14. https://www.jstor.org/stable/41175922.

"Humani Generis (August 12, 1950) | PIUS XII." Accessed January 18, 2022. https://www.vatican.va/content/pius-xii/en/encyclicals/documents/hf_p-xii_enc_12081950_humani-generis.html.

Hynson, Lawrence M. "Religion, Attendance, and Belief in an Afterlife," 1975. https://doi.org/10.2307/1384910.

Kasonde, Chikonde. "Joseph Ratzinger's Reflection on The Immortality of the Soul." Accessed November 23, 2021. https://www.academia.edu/45123780/Joseph_Ratzinger_s_Reflection_on_The_Immortality_of_the_Soul.

Keogh, Gary. "Theology After New Atheism." *New Blackfriars* 96, no. 1066 (2015): 739–50. https://www.jstor.org/stable/24766379.

Khan, Muhammad M., trans. *The Translation of the Meanings of Summarized Sahih Al-Bukhari: Arabic-English*. Lahore, Pakistan? Dar-us-Salam Publications, 1995.

King, D. E., and B. Bushwick. "Beliefs and Attitudes of Hospital Inpatients about Faith Healing and Prayer." *The Journal of Family Practice* 39, no. 4 (October 1994): 349–52.

King, J. Norman, and Barry L. Whitney. "Rahner and Hartshorne on Death and Eternal Life." *Horizons* 15, no. 2 (1988): 239–61. https://doi.org/10.1017/S0360966900039141.

King, Nicholas, Stuart Nelson, Samuel Joseph, Mahveesh Chowdhury, Benjamin Whitfield, Pahul Hanjra, and Lawrence O. Lin. "The Sacred Sites of Houston: A Novel Experiential Course for Undergraduate Medical Education on Religion and Spirituality." *Journal of Religion and Health* 60, no. 6 (December 2021): 4500–4520. https://doi.org/10.1007/s10943-021-01325-3.

Kunapuli, Sanjay, Salvatore Rosanio, and Ernst R. Schwarz. "'How Do Cardiomyocytes Die?' Apoptosis and Autophagic Cell Death in Cardiac Myocytes." *Journal of Cardiac Failure* 12, no. 5 (June 2006): 381–91. https://doi.org/10.1016/j.cardfail.2006.02.002.

Küng, Hans. *Ewiges Leben?* Neuauflage, Nachdruck. München: Piper, 2002.

Kurzweil, Ray. *The Singularity Is Near: When Humans Transcend Biology.* New York: Penguin Books, 2006.

Kwon, Seong Gyu, Yang Woo Kwon, Tae Wook Lee, Gyu Tae Park, and Jae Ho Kim. "Recent Advances in Stem Cell Therapeutics and Tissue Engineering Strategies." *Biomaterials Research* 22 (2018): 36. https://doi.org/10.1186/s40824-018-0148-4.

Ledermann, E. K. "Dogmas Of Medicine." *The British Medical Journal* 1, no. 4548 (1948): 476–476. https://www.jstor.org/stable/25362755.

Lee, Byung-Chul, and Kyung-Rok Yu. "Impact of Mesenchymal Stem Cell Senescence on Inflammaging." *BMB Reports* 53, no. 2 (February 2020): 65–73.

Levin, J. S., D. B. Larson, and C. M. Puchalski. "Religion and Spirituality in Medicine: Research and Education." *JAMA* 278, no. 9 (September 3, 1997): 792–93. https://doi.org/10.1001/jama.278.9.792.

Hindustan Times. "Live Longer, Healthier like This 120-Year-Old Varanasi Monk in 5 Easy Steps," August 19, 2016. https://www.hindustantimes.com/health-and-fitness/live-longer-healthier-like-this-120-year-old-varanasi-monk-in-5-easy-steps/story-pVk5Xd9NcI624RRkb25muL.html.

BioLogos. "Long Life Spans in Genesis: Literal or Symbolic? - Articles." Accessed January 12, 2022. https://biologos.org/articles/long-life-spans-in-genesis-literal-or-symbolic/.

López-Tarrida, Ángela Del Carmen, Rocío de Diego-Cordero, and Joaquin Salvador Lima-Rodríguez. "Spirituality in a Doctor's Practice: What Are the Issues?" *Journal of Clinical Medicine* 10, no. 23 (November 29, 2021): 5612. https://doi.org/10.3390/jcm10235612.

Machado, C. *Brain Death: A Reappraisal.* 2007th edition. Springer, 2014.

Macmillan, Patrick, and Stephen A. Geraci. "Culture Shift: Building an Awareness of Our Mortality." *Cureus* 9, no. 12 (December 20, 2017): e1969. https://doi.org/10.7759/cureus.1969.

Maddox, J. "The Prevalent Distrust of Science." *Nature* 378, no. 6556 (November 30, 1995): 435–37. https://doi.org/10.1038/378435a0.

"Marquis de Condorcet | Biography, Writings, & Facts | Britannica." Accessed January 17, 2022. https://www.britannica.com/biography/

Marie-Jean-Antoine-Nicolas-de-Caritat-marquis-de-Condorcet
#ref272135.

Masic, Izet. "On Occasion of 800th Anniversary of Birth of Ibn Al-Naf-
is--Discoverer of Cardiac and Pulmonary Circulation." *Medicinski
Arhiv* 64, no. 5 (2010): 309–13. https://doi.org/10.5455/
medarh.2010.64.309-313.

May, Todd. *Death*. 1st edition. Stocksfield: Routledge, 2014.

Mayor, Susan. "Sixty Seconds on . . . Cryopreservation." *BMJ: British Medical Journal* 355 (2016). https://www.jstor.org/stable/26947795.

McDermott, John M. "The Christologies of Karl Rahner - II." *Gregorianum*
67, no. 2 (1986): 297–327. https://www.jstor.org/stable/23577184.

McInerny, Ralph, and John O'Callaghan. "Saint Thomas Aquinas." In
The Stanford Encyclopedia of Philosophy, edited by Edward N. Zalta,
Summer 2018. Metaphysics Research Lab, Stanford University, 2018.
https://plato.stanford.edu/archives/sum2018/entries/aquinas/.

"MEDICAL THEOLOGY." *Journal of the American Medical Association*
XXXIV, no. 17 (April 28, 1900): 1075. https://doi.org/10.1001/
jama.1900.02460170055012.

Meyer, Stephen C. *Darwin's Doubt: The Explosive Origin of Animal Life
and the Case for Intelligent Design*. Revised ed. edition. New York, NY:
HarperOne, 2014.

Mishra, Sundeep. "Does Modern Medicine Increase Life-Expectancy:
Quest for the Moon Rabbit?" *Indian Heart Journal* 68, no. 1 (February
2016): 19–27. https://doi.org/10.1016/j.ihj.2016.01.003.

Mukundananda, Swami. "Chapter 2, Verse 20 – Bhagavad Gita, The Song
of God – Swami Mukundananda." Accessed November 23, 2021.
https://www.holy-bhagavad-gita.org/chapter/2/verse/20.

Murphy, Nancey. "Immortality versus Resurrection in the Christian
Tradition." *Annals of the New York Academy of Sciences* 1234 (October
2011): 76–82. https://doi.org/10.1111/j.1749-6632.2011.06132.x.

Naghi, Jesse J., Kiran J. Philip, Anita Phan, Laurent Cleenewerck, and
Ernst R. Schwarz. "The Effects of Spirituality and Religion on Outcomes in Patients with Chronic Heart Failure." *Journal of Religion and*

Health 51, no. 4 (December 2012): 1124–36. https://doi.org/10.1007/ s10943-010-9419-7.

Nietzsche, Friedrich. *The Gay Science: With a Prelude in Rhymes and an Appendix of Songs*. Translated by Walter Kaufmann. 1st edition. New York: Vintage, 1974.

Nimmo, Paul T. *The Oxford Handbook of Karl Barth*. Oxford University Press, 2020.

Noegel, Scott B. "GOD OF HEAVEN AND SHEOL: THE 'UNEARTH-ING' OF CREATION." *Hebrew Studies* 58 (2017): 119–44. https:// www.jstor.org/stable/26304263.

OP, Aidan Nichols. *The Shape of Catholic Theology: An Introduction to Its Sources, Principles, and History*. Collegeville, Minn: Liturgical Press, 1991.

O'Regan, Cyril. "Benedict XVI: Eschatology as Mirror and Lamp." Church Life Journal. Accessed April 2, 2022. https://churchlifejournal.nd.edu/ articles/benedict-xvi-eschatology-as-mirror-and-lamp/.

Palmer, John. *The Method of Hypothesis and the Nature of Soul in Plato's Phaedo*. Cambridge University Press, 2021.

Pandya, Sunil K. "Understanding Brain, Mind and Soul: Contributions from Neurology and Neurosurgery." *Mens Sana Monographs* 9, no. 1 (January 2011): 129–49. https://doi.org/10.4103/0973-1229.77431.

Pedersen, Esther Oluffa. "RELIGION IS THE OPIUM OF THE PEOPLE: AN INVESTIGATION INTO THE INTELLECTUAL CONTEXT OF MARX'S CRITIQUE OF RELIGION." *History of Political Thought* 36, no. 2 (2015): 354–87. https://www.jstor.org/ stable/26228603.

Pembroke, Neil Francis. "Appropriate Spiritual Care by Physicians: A Theo-logical Perspective." *Journal of Religion and Health* 47, no. 4 (Decem-ber 2008): 549–59. https://doi.org/10.1007/s10943-008-9183-0.

Pettus, Maude. "PERMANENCE." The Christian Science Journal, December 1, 1937. https://journal.christianscience.com/shared/ view/2eqvu4kjwys?s=f.

NBC News. "Pope: Creation vs. Evolution Clash an 'Absurdity.'" Accessed January 18, 2022. https://www.nbcnews.com/id/wbna19956961.

Pound, Richard W., and Andy Miah. "Human Enhancement." *Issues in Science and Technology* 25, no. 4 (2009): 5–8. https://www.jstor.org/stable/43314896.

Pulciani, Simonetta, and Emanuele Nutile. "[Relationships between Medicine and Spirituality]." *Giornale Italiano Di Nefrologia: Organo Ufficiale Della Societa Italiana Di Nefrologia* 36, no. 1 (February 2019): 2019-vol1.

Putz, Oliver. "Evolutionary Biology in the Theology of Karl Rahner." *Philosophy and Theology* 17, no. 1/2 (July 1, 2005): 85–105. https://doi.org/10.5840/philtheol2005171/25.

Rachello, Olga, and Mark O'Connell. "Lives of the Immortalists." *The New Atlantis*, no. 54 (2018): 113–19. https://www.jstor.org/stable/90021012.

Rahner, Karl. *The Content of Faith: The Best of Karl Rahner's Theological Writings*. Reprint edition. New York, NY: Herder & Herder, 2013.

———. *Theological Investigations Volume IV*. New York: Herder & Herder, 1973.

Rando, Thomas A., and Howard Y. Chang. "Aging, Rejuvenation, and Epigenetic Reprogramming: Resetting the Aging Clock." *Cell* 148, no. 1–2 (January 20, 2012): 46–57. https://doi.org/10.1016/j.cell.2012.01.003.

Ratzinger, Joseph. *Jesus von Nazareth*. Verlag Herder, 2017.

"R.E. Roberts, The Theology of Tertullian (1924), Chapter 11 (Pp.203-218)." Accessed November 23, 2021. https://www.tertullian.org/articles/roberts_theology/roberts_11.htm.

"Reflexions on Death - Sebastian Moore, 1952." Accessed November 23, 2021. https://journals.sagepub.com/doi/abs/10.1177/001258065207022202.

Remshardt, Ralf. "Posthumanism." In *Mapping Intermediality in Performance*, edited by Sarah Bay-Cheng, Chiel Kattenbelt, Andy Lavender, and Robin Nelson, 135–39. Amsterdam University Press, 2010. https://www.jstor.org/stable/j.ctt46mwjd.24.

Return of the God Hypothesis. Accessed March 26, 2022. https://bookoutlet.com/products/9780062071507B/return-of-the-god-hypothesis?-

source=ppc&ppc_campaign=PLA-US&keyword=&gclid=Cj0KC-Qjw8_qRBhCXARIsAE2AtRaCzRH-Oe1bdQr3kZw9nVE6pz7P-0Wq39sbWwua8vp-j9ouKUnyCemsaAnsjEALw_wcB.

Ritchie, A. D. "Theories of Immortality." *Philosophy* 17, no. 66 (1942): 117–27. https://www.jstor.org/stable/3747301.

Romito, Antonio, and Gilda Cobellis. "Pluripotent Stem Cells: Current Understanding and Future Directions." *Stem Cells International* 2016 (2016): 9451492. https://doi.org/10.1155/2016/9451492.

Rowell, James L. *Making Sense of the Sacred: The Meaning of World Religions*. Fortress Press, 2021.

Russo, Marc A., Danielle M. Santarelli, and Dean O'Rourke. "The Physiological Effects of Slow Breathing in the Healthy Human." *Breathe (Sheffield, England)* 13, no. 4 (December 2017): 298–309. https://doi.org/10.1183/20734735.009817.

Ryan, John A. *Science and Spirituality*. Mzuni Press, 2016. https://doi.org/10.2307/j.ctvh8r1jq.

Sanada, Fumihiro, Yoshiaki Taniyama, Jun Muratsu, Rei Otsu, Hideo Shimizu, Hiromi Rakugi, and Ryuichi Morishita. "Source of Chronic Inflammation in Aging." *Frontiers in Cardiovascular Medicine* 5 (2018): 12. https://doi.org/10.3389/fcvm.2018.00012.

Says, Seo Specialist. "Science, Religion, and Secularism Part VI: Jonathan Hedley Brooke, Complexity Thesis | The Partially Examined Life Philosophy Podcast | A Philosophy Podcast and Blog," October 18, 2017. https://partiallyexaminedlife.com/2017/10/18/science-religion-and-secularism-part-vi-jonathan-hedley-brooke-complexity-thesis/.

Scanlan, James P. "Dostoevsky's Arguments for Immortality." *The Russian Review* 59, no. 1 (2000): 1–20. https://www.jstor.org/stable/2679619.

"Schrödinger's Cat." In *Wikipedia*, April 2, 2022. https://en.wikipedia.org/w/index.php?title=Schr%C3%B6dinger%27s_cat&oldid=1080709331.

Schuh, Alexander, Sebastian Breuer, Raja Al Dashti, Nasir Sulemanjee, Peter Hanrath, Christian Weber, Barry F. Uretsky, and Ernst R. Schwarz. "Administration of Vascular Endothelial Growth Factor

Adjunctive to Fetal Cardiomyocyte Transplantation and Improvement of Cardiac Function in the Rat Model." *Journal of Cardiovascular Pharmacology and Therapeutics* 10, no. 1 (March 2005): 55–66. https://doi.org/10.1177/107424840501000107.

Schwarz, E. R., J. Schaper, J. vom Dahl, C. Altehoefer, B. Grohmann, F. Schoendube, F. H. Sheehan, et al. "Myocyte Degeneration and Cell Death in Hibernating Human Myocardium." *Journal of the American College of Cardiology* 27, no. 7 (June 1996): 1577–85. https://doi.org/10.1016/0735-1097(96)00059-9.

Schwarz, Ernst R., Kiran J. Philip, Sinan A. Simsir, Lawrence Czer, Alfredo Trento, Stuart G. Finder, and Laurent A. Cleenewerck. "Maximal Care Considerations When Treating Patients with End-Stage Heart Failure: Ethical and Procedural Quandaries in Management of the Very Sick." *Journal of Religion and Health* 50, no. 4 (December 2011): 872–79. https://doi.org/10.1007/s10943-010-9326-y.

———. "Maximal Care Considerations When Treating Patients with End-Stage Heart Failure: Ethical and Procedural Quandaries in Management of the Very Sick." *Journal of Religion and Health* 50, no. 4 (December 2011): 872–79. https://doi.org/10.1007/s10943-010-9326-y.

Schwarz, Ernst R., and Salvatore Rosanio. "Religion and the Catholic Church's View on (Heart) Transplantation: A Recent Statement of Pope Benedict XVI and Its Practical Impact." *Journal of Religion and Health* 50, no. 3 (September 2011): 564–74. https://doi.org/10.1007/s10943-009-9284-4.

Schwarz, Ernst von. *The Secret World of Stem Cell Therapy: What YOU Need to Know about the Health, Beauty, and Anti-Aging Breakthrough.* Morgan James Publishing, 2022.

Shay, J. W., and W. E. Wright. "Hayflick, His Limit, and Cellular Ageing." *Nature Reviews. Molecular Cell Biology* 1, no. 1 (October 2000): 72–76. https://doi.org/10.1038/35036093.

Siegel, Ethan. "No, Science Will Never Make Philosophy Or Religion Obsolete." Forbes. Accessed January 19, 2022. https://www.forbes.

com/sites/startswithabang/2020/06/30/no-science-will-never-make-philosophy-or-religion-obsolete/.

Simpson, Ain, and Kimberly Rios. "Is Science for Atheists? Perceived Threat to Religious Cultural Authority Explains U.S. Christians' Distrust in Secularized Science." *Public Understanding of Science (Bristol, England)* 28, no. 7 (October 2019): 740–58. https://doi.org/10.1177/0963662519871881.

Sipe, J. D., and A. S. Cohen. "Review: History of the Amyloid Fibril." *Journal of Structural Biology* 130, no. 2–3 (June 2000): 88–98. https://doi.org/10.1006/jsbi.2000.4221.

Skobel, Erik, Alexander Schuh, Ernst R. Schwarz, Elisa A. Liehn, Andreas Franke, Sebastian Breuer, Kalle Günther, Thorsten Reffelmann, Peter Hanrath, and Christian Weber. "Transplantation of Fetal Cardiomyocytes into Infarcted Rat Hearts Results in Long-Term Functional Improvement." *Tissue Engineering* 10, no. 5–6 (June 2004): 849–64. https://doi.org/10.1089/1076327041348491.

Stenvinkel, Peter, and Paul G. Shiels. "Long-Lived Animals with Negligible Senescence: Clues for Ageing Research." *Biochemical Society Transactions* 47, no. 4 (August 30, 2019): 1157–64. https://doi.org/10.1042/BST20190105.

"Stephen Hawking: Stephen Hawking Warned Artificial Intelligence Could End Human Race - The Economic Times." Accessed August 24, 2021. https://economictimes.indiatimes.com/news/science/stephen-hawking-warned-artificial-intelligence-could-end-human-race/articleshow/63297552.cms?from=mdr.

Straus, Marc J. "Alchemy." *Ploughshares* 30, no. 4 (2004): 144–144. https://www.jstor.org/stable/40355006.

Takahashi, Kazutoshi, and Shinya Yamanaka. "Induction of Pluripotent Stem Cells from Mouse Embryonic and Adult Fibroblast Cultures by Defined Factors." *Cell* 126, no. 4 (August 25, 2006): 663–76. https://doi.org/10.1016/j.cell.2006.07.024.

"The Case for Conditional Immortality - J. W. Wenham." Accessed December 2, 2021. https://www.truthaccordingtoscripture.com/documents/death/conditional-immortality-wenham.php#.YakvsNnMJQI.

"The Catholic Church Is Losing Its Most Devoted Followers | HuffPost Null." Accessed January 17, 2022. https://www.huffpost.com/entry/opinion-catholic-church-native-latino_n_5b-969d89e4b0162f472fb4bb.

The Epic of Gilgamesh: An English Verison with an Introduction. Penguin, 1960.

The History of Christian Theology. Accessed April 2, 2022. https://www.audible.com/pd/The-History-of-Christian-Theology-Audiobook/B00DEK2MWC.

The Legend of the Wandering Jew. Accessed September 7, 2021. https://press.uchicago.edu/ucp/books/book/distributed/L/bo44306613.html.

"The Singularity Is Nearer - by Ray Kurzweil (Hardcover)." Accessed January 8, 2022. https://www.target.com/p/the-singularity-is-nearer-by-ray-kurzweil-hardcover/-/A-84104039.

Thompson, Kathryn, Hyo Jung Tak, Magdy El-Din, Syed Madani, Simon G. Brauer, and John D. Yoon. "Physicians' Religious Characteristics and Their Perceptions of the Psychological Impact of Patient Prayer and Beliefs at the End of Life: A National Survey." *The American Journal of Hospice & Palliative Care* 36, no. 2 (February 2019): 116–22. https://doi.org/10.1177/1049909118792871.

ThriftBooks. "A Brief Introduction to Hinduism:... Book by Arthur Herman." ThriftBooks. Accessed November 23, 2021. https://www.thriftbooks.com/w/a-brief-introduction-to-hinduism-religion-philosophy-and-ways-of-liberation_arthur-herman_al-herman/922264/.

———. "Ending Aging: The Rejuvenation... Book by Aubrey de Grey." ThriftBooks. Accessed November 23, 2021. https://www.thriftbooks.com/w/ending-aging-the-rejuvenation-biotechnologies-that-could-reverse-human-aging-in-our-lifetime_aubrey-de-grey_michael-rae/709587/.

———. "Eternal Life? Life after Death As a... Book by Hans Küng." ThriftBooks. Accessed November 24, 2021. https://www.thriftbooks.com/w/eternal-life-life-after-death-as-a-medical-philosophi-cal-and-theological-problem_hans-kng/573635/.

————. "The Denial Of Death Book by Ernest Becker." ThriftBooks. Accessed November 23, 2021. https://www.thriftbooks.com/w/the-denial-of-death_daniel-goleman_ernest-becker/255140/.

————. "Theological Investigations V22 Book by Karl Rahner." Thrift-Books. Accessed November 24, 2021. https://www.thriftbooks.com/w/theological-investigations-v22_karl-rahner/13658297/.

Tolahunase, Madhuri, Rajesh Sagar, and Rima Dada. "Impact of Yoga and Meditation on Cellular Aging in Apparently Healthy Individuals: A Prospective, Open-Label Single-Arm Exploratory Study." *Oxidative Medicine and Cellular Longevity* 2017 (2017): 7928981. https://doi.org/10.1155/2017/7928981.

Torre, Lindsey A., Rebecca L. Siegel, Elizabeth M. Ward, and Ahmedin Jemal. "Global Cancer Incidence and Mortality Rates and Trends--An Update." *Cancer Epidemiology, Biomarkers & Prevention: A Publication of the American Association for Cancer Research, Cosponsored by the American Society of Preventive Oncology* 25, no. 1 (January 2016): 16–27. https://doi.org/10.1158/1055-9965.EPI-15-0578.

"Transformed By the Light: The Powerful Effect of Near-Death Experiences on People's Lives by Dr. Melvin L. Morse: GOOD Hardcover (1992) | Free Shipping Books." Accessed March 22, 2022. https://www.abebooks.com/9780679404439/Transformed-Light-Powerful-Effect-Near-Death-0679404430/plp.

Trounson, A. O. "Cryopreservation." *British Medical Bulletin* 46, no. 3 (July 1990): 695–708. https://doi.org/10.1093/oxfordjournals.bmb.a072425.

University of Oxford. *Richard Dawkins versus Rowan Williams: Humanity's Ultimate Origins*, 2012. https://www.youtube.com/watch?v=zruhc7X-qSxo.

Uniwersytet w Białymstoku, and Andrzej Proniewski. "Joseph Ratzinger's Philosophical Theology of the Person." *Rocznik Teologii Katolickiej* 17, no. 3 (2018): 219–36. https://doi.org/10.15290/rtk.2018.17.3.16.

USERID43. "Victor Stenger, 1935 – 2014 - Freedom From Religion Foundation." Accessed January 15, 2022. https://ffrf.org/publications/freethought-today/item/21586-victor-stenger-1935-2014.

Uveges, Melissa Kurtz, Jill B. Hamilton, Kelli DePriest, Renee Boss, Pamela S. Hinds, and Marie T. Nolan. "The Influence of Parents' Religiosity or Spirituality on Decision Making for Their Critically Ill Child: An Integrative Review." *Journal of Palliative Medicine* 22, no. 11 (November 2019): 1455–67. https://doi.org/10.1089/jpm.2019.0154.

V, Jayaram. "The Four Yugas and Their Significance." Accessed November 23, 2021. https://www.hinduwebsite.com/timecycle.asp.

"Von Der Unbegreiflichkeit Gottes. Erfahrungen Eines Katholischen Theologen Geisteswissenschaften Religion Theologie Christentum Glaube Philosophie Christliche Religionen Rahner, Karl Theologe Karl Rahner, Albert Raffelt Und Karl Lehmann Herder Verlag Erstmals Als Buchveröffentlichung Karl Rahners Letzte Große Rede. In Seinen 'Erfahrungen Eines Theologen' Fasst Karl Rahner Die Anleigen Seines Theologischen Lebens Zusammen Und Lässt Zugleich in Sein Herz Blickenein Geistliches Testament Für Das 21. Jahrhundert. Autor Karl Rahner SJ, 1904 -1984; Lehrtätigkeit in Innsbruck, München Und Münster. Er Ist Einer Der Bedeutenden Theologen Des 20.Jahrhunderts Und Ein Großer Spiritueller Lehrer. Albert Raffelt, Dr. Theol., Geb. 1944, Ist Bibliotheksdirektor a. D. Und Honorarprofessor Für Dogmatische Theologie an Der Universität Freiburg i. Br.Prof. Dr. Phil. Dr. Theol. Karl Kardinal Lehmann, Geboren 1936, Ist Bischof von Mainz Und War von 1987 Bis 2008 Vorsitzender Der Deutschen Bischofskonferenz. by Karl Rahner Dr. Theol. Albert Raffelt Bibliotheksdirektor a. D. Honorarprofessor Für Dogmatische Theologie Universität Freiburg i. Br. Prof. Dr. Phil. Dr. Theol. Karl Kardinal Lehmann: Gut Softcover (2004) Auflage: 4. | BUCHSERVICE / ANTIQUARIAT Lars Lutzer." Accessed January 13, 2022. https://www.abebooks.com/Unbegreiflichkeit-Gottes-Erfahrungen-katholischen-Theologen-Geisteswissenschaften/7113670353/bd.

Walter, Chip. *Immortality, Inc.: Renegade Science, Silicon Valley Billions, and the Quest to Live Forever*. National Geographic Books, 2020.

Wang, Wuzhou, Yun Ma, Junyan He, Huizhou Qi, Fangzhu Xiao, and Shuya He. "Gene Regulation for the Extreme Resistance to Ionizing Radiation of Deinococcus Radiodurans." *Gene* 715 (October 5, 2019): 144008. https://doi.org/10.1016/j.gene.2019.144008.

Westman, Robert. *The Copernican Question: Prognostication, Skepticism, and Celestial Order*. Univ of California Press, 2020.

Wiker, Benjamin. *The Catholic Church & Science: Answering the Questions, Exposing the Myths*. TAN Books, 2011.

Wolf-Meyer, Matthew J. *Theory for the World to Come: Speculative Fiction and Apocalyptic Anthropology*. U of Minnesota Press, 2019.

About the Author

D r. Ernst R. von Schwarz, MD, PhD is an Austrian-German-American physician and researcher who is a descendent of a Austrian-German family consisting of more than twenty doctors of medicine throughout the centuries. He grew up in Germany and received his Venia Legendi (Professor of Medicine) at the RWTH University of Technology in Aachen/Germany. He is a triple board-certified internist, cardiologist, and heart transplant cardiologist in Los Angeles. He is also a Professor of Medicine at Cedars Sinai Medical Center and a Clinical Professor at the David Geffen School of Medicine at UCLA and UC Riverside. Dr. Schwarz is a world-renowned clinical and academic heart specialist and serves as the Director of Cardiology and Director of the Heart Institute of the Southern California Hospital in Los Angeles, as well as Director and President of the Pacific Heart Medical Group in Murrieta, CEO of Dr. Schwarz Medical Institute of California, and Medical Director of HeartStem, Inc.

Dr. Schwarz has published more than 150 scientific articles in international, peer-reviewed journals, several book chapters, and books in cardiology and medicine. He is a sought-after speaker at international scientific conferences worldwide. Dr. Schwarz is one of the thought leaders in modern future technologies, including stem cell therapies for chronic diseases for the heart and other organs. Students from universities from all over the world seek internships with Dr. Schwarz on an ongoing basis.

Dr. Schwarz studied medicine at the Universities of Vienna in Austria and the Philipps University in Marburg, Germany, and he worked and earned academic positions at the RWTH University of Technology in Aachen, Germany, the University of Ife in Ile-Ife in Nigeria, a Harvard affiliated hospital in Jeddah, Saudi Arabia, the University of Texas in Galveston, Texas, and Cedars Sinai Medical Center and UCLA. He resides in Los Angeles and Germany and has clinical practices in Los Angeles, Culver City, and Temecula, California.

For over 10 years, Dr. Schwarz has studied Roman Catholic Theology via EUCLID University and finished his thesis on the theological and medical views on immortality and everlasting life in April 2022. He also is Professor of Bioethics at Euclid University since 2022.

A free ebook edition is available with the purchase of this book.

To claim your free ebook edition:

1. Visit MorganJamesBOGO.com
2. Sign your name CLEARLY in the space
3. Complete the form and submit a photo of the entire copyright page
4. You or your friend can download the ebook to your preferred device

A **FREE** ebook edition is available for you or a friend with the purchase of this print book.

CLEARLY SIGN YOUR NAME ABOVE

Instructions to claim your free ebook edition:
1. Visit MorganJamesBOGO.com
2. Sign your name CLEARLY in the space above
3. Complete the form and submit a photo of this entire page
4. You or your friend can download the ebook to your preferred device

Print & Digital Together Forever.

Snap a photo

Free ebook

Read anywhere

CPSIA information can be obtained
at www.ICGtesting.com
Printed in the USA
JSHW020339010723
44072JS00001B/2

9 781636 980805